The Road from Oz

The Road from Oz

Dorothy Canote

Compass Flower Press
Columbia, Missouri

Compass
Flower
Press

Published by Compass Flower Press
Columbia, MO 65203

Compass
Flower
Press

Library of Congress Control Number: 2023910988

ISBN: 978-1-951960-49-0

Cover painting: *Oak Savannah*

Acknowledgment

When I began my modest literary career, I was extremely fortunate to have found a wonderful guide. I wish to thank my editor and publisher, Yolanda Ciolli for her help in assembling and publishing my work. I greatly value her insight in helping me say what I really mean, her patience with my resistance to revision, and most of all her friendship. All writers should be so lucky.

Dedication

This, my third book of paintings and essays, is dedicated to the kind, delightfully uninhibited, and party–loving gals in my watercolor group, The Ladies Love to Paint. We have been together for some years now, gaining and losing some members, but never losing touch. We rarely miss a Tuesday together, and with their friendship and support my life has been enriched beyond expression.

Table of Contents

Preface

I was born in Oz. No, wait. I was born in Chicago. But when I search my memories, I was born into a world like Oz, of brightness and wonder. And I walked a path that might as well have been paved with golden bricks, because it led through days and months and years of beautiful and subtle adventures.

But I feel I should preface the writing that follows with disclaimers. Of course I don't remember all the ouchies, the bumps and bruises, the disappointments, the fears and scars, literal and figurative, that paved that bright path. And it hasn't been all light and laughter, because what fool would believe that? But while I have many regrets, I have little to complain of and very, very much to be thankful for.

When I began this, my third book of watercolor essays, I had to work harder to pull out some of the events and small adventures of my past that I thought might appeal to readers. And I found myself having to dig deeper into myself and think harder about what lay below the superficial memories of my life.

The road from Oz has been like a ride on an old, slow train, with me looking out the window between stops, getting off for excursions into new territories, meeting fellow travelers along the way. The stories, the memories, are souvenirs from the stops. It doesn't seem like it was a long trip. Where did the time go? And I saw so much! Born in 1946, the slow days of my childhood and youth, the 1950s and the 1960s, seem as clear and recent as yesterday, and so much happened in the world in those years. After that, time flew by like water down the mighty Missouri River, steady and undeterred, busy and full.

These days most but I hope not all of the adventures and delightful surprises of my life are behind me. While I am frustrated with the limitations of an aging body, I won't belabor the complaints and indignities that keep me from the active outdoor life I used to enjoy. But as I sit on my front porch or similar restful perch and let my mind loose from to–do lists, I find myself being more in the moment, enjoying the depth and vibrancy of color in the birds, insects, trees and flowers, the sun and sky. The scents of nearby blossoms, the grass—just cut or drying in the end–of–summer sun—and earth wet from a recent rain, all bring back to me the stops along the road from Oz.

Chapter One
Mother Earth

My mother would proverbially, not roll over in but rise up from her grave if she knew, but the fact is that both my daughters and myself are in one sense or another pagan. Well, I personally haven't entirely forsaken the religion of my ancestors, but I do worship a lot differently these days. One daughter is actually a practicing pagan, while the other comes closer to agnosticism. But all three of us worship at the alter of Mother Earth, all three of us are naturalists in one form or another. Jennifer is a landscaper, her own boss and queen of her horticultural realm; Angela works for Texas Parks and Wildlife as an invasive species biologist. I like to think of them as wonderful fruit that didn't fall far from the tree.

Of all the abiding truths of my life, I am most grateful for those revealed to me by the natural world. While nature holds unrivaled beauty, its methods are not necessarily benign. Life for most organisms is a constant struggle for the necessities, and death is a natural part of that struggle. Only we humans have the foolishness to think we are somehow different. If anything, we are more often a detriment than a benefit to other living creatures.

Still, as a sentient species it is inevitable that we will try to find some meaning in our existence. Otherwise what excuse do we have for our hubris? So let me just share a few of my own thoughts on the subject, and some of my experiences with the Goddess.

Wind

The wind has blown unceasingly the last three days, somewhat unusual for the end of May. My husband James is cheerful and positive. "This wind will dry the hay fields!" he says. That's not an insignificant observation when you live on a farm. Like vegetables in the garden, it is important to harvest grasses when the leaves are at a point of maximum nutrition and palatability, before they put all their energy into the seed. Once the hay is down (cut), if it rains on it before it can cure, it has to be left to dry again before it can be baled.

Between the wind and rain, farming is always a crap shoot. Too much rain can prevent spring planting or fall harvest or too little rain may come when crops are growing. If farmers had the personality and constitution of bankers, merchants, and politicians they would have constantly bleeding ulcers. Of course, these days maybe everyone is prone to bleeding ulcers.

When I was growing for the farmers market, aka market gardening, I hated windy days. Something about the friction of the air made me want to go to the house. My landscaper daughter, Jennifer, agrees with me and also hates to work in the wind. I have read that in the southeast of Europe, when

the sirocco winds blow north from the arid regions of northern Africa, law enforcement notes an increase in violent crimes, and the rate of murder and suicide increases.

In my travels across the Great Plains states I have had occasion to step out of the car to better experience the vast spaces, unbroken and unobscured by trees as they are in Missouri. The winds blow relentlessly across those spaces, and I recalled the 1988 novel by Glendon Swarthout, *The Homesman*. While the definition of homesman was not in my Websters Ninth New Collegiate Dictionary, the term was apparently coined and generally used in the 1800s. Men were hired to return female settlers who were physically broken down or mentally disturbed from their prairie homesteads back east to relatives or establishments devoted to their care. I could appreciate that the wind probably drove them crazy.

The relentless motion of the air is very like the pace of life these days, events and people rushing by too fast to make sense of what they mean or portend. I think kids especially suffer by having too much flying at them, not enough time to observe and think about the world and their lives and who they are or wish to become. It's no wonder young people pick up guns and try to destroy what they don't understand.

Until I retired, I couldn't appreciate how soothing it is to have the leisure of watching the birds nest, or the grass grow, or . . . the wind blow.

3

Desert flash flood

Water

I'm a Pisces. Barely. If I were born a couple of days earlier I would be an Aquarius. This means I'm on the cusp between two astrological signs. Both are water signs. If you're not into astrology you can just skip this part. However, if you are also like me, a semi-believer, you will realize that we Pisces have a tendency toward mysticism. I like to believe this attribute is what makes me a nature girl.

I've always been drawn to water, but also a little afraid of it. Growing up smack in the center of the North American continent I never saw the ocean until I chaperoned a senior class trip to Galveston in 1976. Neither the day nor the ocean there was beautiful—shades of gray, wind blowing, waves pounding the seawall—and it didn't take long to get enough of it.

It's pretty easy to take water for granted, especially if you live where there is plenty of it. However, it's not the availability of water I want to write about, because everyone knows instinctively that water is a critical necessity for life. Rather, it's the properties of water that amaze me.

Biological Water—The Microzone

I'd like to pass along some of the concerns I have about the impact humans have on the water we take for granted. This involves a bit of non–chemical chemistry, so bear with me a bit.

Water dissolves things. Not all things, but enough. Neither metal or nonmetals dissolve readily in water, but if a substance can form charged particles—ions—those ions are attracted to water molecules that can carry them around, especially if the water also has acid in it. Substances that dissolve then have a medium, a soup, where they can react with each other. That is how and where life processes occur—in the soup. I don't think I'll write any more about that because it makes me hungry.

However, I do think a lot about the soup of the world, or it might be better to describe it as the lagoon of the world. All the waste of the world has been dumped into the water as long as we have had waste to dispose of. That wasn't too bad as long as there weren't too many people dumping and the stuff they dumped was biodegradable. The decomposer microbes made a great living from it. But since the chemical revolution of the 1900s, the soup ingredients have gotten more and more complex.

We mostly think when we flush the toilet all that waste goes to the treatment plant and gets magically cleaned up before it goes back into the environment. And most of it does, but what doesn't can become problematic.

Take pharmaceuticals. When you pop a pill, the active ingredient in many cases passes through your gut where it gets its nice little coating dissolved and is absorbed into the blood. The problem is that many drugs are poorly absorbed, so maybe more than 90% of the dose passes on through and gets flushed down the toilet, passes unaltered through the treatment process, and is released into the environment, where it 'doses' the little critters that live in the water. Those organisms make up the base of an aquatic food chain, and the chemical may either kill them or be bioaccumulated and passed up the food chain, increasingly concentrating at each step until there is enough to alter, in various ways, the biology of the system.

I have a few last thoughts about biological water, in case you are lulled into a false sense of security about the wonderful purified bottled water that has become such an integral part of our lives. While the quality of the plastics continues to improve, there is still a whole suite of substances that leach out of the plastic that our bodies could do without. The worst are possibly the estrogen–mimics that are absorbed and travel throughout the body acting like female hormones. The amazing part is that a single molecule is able to act on DNA and turn genes on and off. That's even scarier when you realize that those molecules are acting on reproductive cells before they ever get to the baby stage. Accidental genetic engineering.

Water in the Macrocosm

Macro—that's the big stuff! Visible, slap you in the face, knock you over and drown you! Okay, too much drama? Still the drama of environmental catastrophe makes news, and with global climate patterns going wacko we pay considerable attention to coverage of too much or too little water. Droughts, floods, rising ocean levels are all wreaking increasing havoc on world populations and will require more and more attention in management from the powers that be.

Anyone who has been the victim of flood waters can appreciate the power of water in ways that other people can't. Moving water has an undeniable power. When I was studying agronomy at MU, I shared an office with emeritus professor Dr. C.M. "Woody" Woodruff. Dr. Woodruff was well known for his research in soil chemistry and especially water use in crops. He was a generous and amiable mentor and we had some entertaining discussions in the basement of Mumford Hall.

We were talking about soil erosion one day and I asked him, "How big a rock can water move?" His reply was, basically, any size. Whoa! Baseball size? Basketball size? Boulders? Yes, all of those. What one has to realize that it is the *push* behind moving water that provides the force. If you have carried a gallon of milk or orange juice home from the grocery store you will have a feel for how much water weighs. Then imagine how many gallons of water come down a river or stream under the force of gravity with the weight of all the water upstream pushing behind it. You can't stop it; just get out of the way!

Water is the shaper of our world. As a river ages it changes its course—eroding, depositing, taking stuff away and leaving stuff behind. Waves and tides erode and change coastlines. Waterfalls cut back the bedrock underneath, and the waterfall moves farther and farther upstream. Flooding flushes everything before it, especially flimsy man-made structures—buildings, levees, bridges—leaving behind an altered landscape and centuries of human bones and detritus.

Even more could be said about hurricanes—the double whammy of wind and water—and building in flood plains and on scenic but unstable coastal shores and cliffs, plus the inevitable rise in ocean levels. But just a word to everyone who lives in Missouri and all those other states not threatened by the surfeit or deficit of the water problem. All those people who live in those places that have too little water and are pilfering from non-rechargeable aquifers or distant rivers, and those whose homes and land are falling or washing away into the ocean, those folks are all going to be looking in the near future to relocate and settle in a safer, more hospitable state. And where do you think they might look?

Light and Dark

Light

Light has a lot to be said for it; however I don't intend to belabor the obvious. Well okay, maybe just a little. "In the beginning…" are the first words in the first chapter in what is purportedly the most widely sold book in the world. And scientists agree that it was light in the beginning that started everything else on earth. Photosynthesis begets oxygen and starts food chains and makes things green. I love green. Light lets us avoid or at least attempt to avoid furry things and turtles on the road, and find our way to the grocery store, parties, and the court house. Light stimulates production of vitamin D in mushrooms and our skin. Oh, and most importantly, it helps us read our beloved books!

There. I have now belabored the obvious!

Dark

I prefer light to stay where it belongs, in the daytime. Back home, in the 1950s in the small town of Avalon where I grew up, there were no street lights. I don't even recall many pole lights, unless they had an on/off switch, nor any of the dusk–to–dawn lights that now light up the towns and cities of our nation and the world. At night I could and did go out and look up into a sky that was as dark black as a velvet Elvis picture, with stars that were so bright they actually twinkled.

The house was always dark when I was a kid and I learned to navigate pretty well when sneaking downstairs for a midnight snack. That is until I happened to turn on the kitchen light one night and encountered a humongous hairy wolf spider in the middle of the kitchen floor, probably also looking for a little midnight snack.

Today it is hard to find places on earth where that degree of darkness still exists. To me, it's just unnatural and unsettling to go to bed with lights all over the place. A midnight trip to the bathroom is lit by the programmable thermostat in the hall, the LED light of the phone landline and clocks throughout the house, the computer modem and the charging station for my husband's tablet.

Even when the power goes out, the lights of Columbia twenty miles to the south mark its location. I think it's sad that all the millions of people who live in and around cities never see the full beauty of the night sky. A nighttime view of earth from orbit reveals the extent of civilization in a strangely beautiful black and white display, but gives no indication of the disruption this light pollution causes to the organisms that depend on day/night cycles and celestial navigation for migrations and the biorhythms of their daily lives.

Thankfully, the two neighbors' dusk-to-dawn lights are not visible as long as the trees are in leaf from spring to fall. When we moved to the farm there was a pole light by the driveway, which we seldom if ever turned on. A few years later we had new neighbors who built across the road to our south. When we asked if they planned to put in a night light they were ambivalent. Luckily they were friends so they took it in good humor when James said if they did, he planned to use it for target practice! That's my man!

As I write this it is the first week of June. Just a few nights ago we had a real boomer of a storm—lightning and thunder for what seemed like hours. It woke me up so I decided to make my nightly trip to the loo. The storm was mostly noise with only light rain and mist so I stepped up to the picture window in the living room to watch the light display. What I saw was more amazing than the lightning. The front yard and the twenty-acre field beyond it was a fairyland of fireflies! There must have been hundreds, maybe millions!!! It was a glorious sight. They evidently were loving the humidity of the fresh-mown pasture and the total darkness from the cloud cover. And they were living up to their other name—lightning bugs!

Thyme

Thymus Vulgaris

D. Panote

Chapter Two
My Life with Plants

When you read my essay "Into the Woods," you will realize that trees are my people. Actually, I like plants better than I like a lot of people. Not that I don't like people, it's just that plants are rarely disappointing, except when they fail to grow or become a rank and odious nuisance. Even the stickery plants and the ones that make me itch are just trying to survive. All the plants with thorns, poisons, and bad tastes are using defenses that have evolved to keep them from being eaten.

I spent many hours of my childhood lying on a blanket under the elm trees in my grandma's yard, looking up at the sticky goo seeping from old wounds in the bark, listening to cicadas, birdsong, and leaves rustling, and I sensed even then, that trees would always be the silent and abiding companions of my life.

As a biology major I took classes in botany, ecology, and plant taxonomy and began to gain a new appreciation for the connections and underlying importance of plants to the entire spectrum of life.

Graduate school courses in biochemistry, as well as weed and soil science added a whole new dimension to my understanding of plants. It wasn't until I spent time in the Ozarks that I really began to learn more about the vegetation of woodlands. The friends I made during graduate school were avid outdoors enthusiasts and as I spent time getting to know the flowers and trees of roadsides and woodlands I began to truly appreciate the diversity and characteristics of Missouri's vegetation.

So now let me dip into some of my experiences with the plant world.

Grasslands

Not all of my experiences in field work were actually in the field. During my career as a graduate student I was funded in part by various jobs and stipends. The first of these was a research project drawing together a compendium of the literature on native grasses. In spite of growing up in Missouri and all the time I had spent in, on, and among grass, I didn't have a clue what they were talking about. Weren't all grasses native?

If you have a house with a yard, you probably have grass to mow. If there isn't any grass and you want some, you have several options. You can rough up the ground, spread around some seed and fertilizer, and water the dickens out of it. Then you guard it by fencing out the kids, dogs, and snoopy neighbors, and waiting for something to happen. Or if you have some money to spend, you can order sod—rolls of grass cut out of a sod farm field—and have it unrolled and fitted together and proceed with the guarding, watering, and ... waiting. But pretty as it may be, it is pretty much guaranteed that the grass you seed or the sod you buy is not what came with the locale.

D. Canote

Native Grasses

The original native grasses of North America were species indigenous to the land, the product of evolution and eons of cycles of weather and seasonal fires. When the European pioneers and explorers first saw the bounty of grasses and wildlife of Virginia, Kentucky, and other eastern states, they were undoubtedly in awe. The woodlands and grasslands supported wild grazers like deer, elk, and bison, as well as turkey, grouse, and the well–known suite of North American predators—wolves, bears, coyotes, and foxes.

In more mountainous eastern areas, especially whose with shallow soils, grasses were often interspersed with trees in associations called savannas. The painting here is of an oak savanna, part woods and part grasses. These are more common east of the Mississippi, extending to the eastern mountain ranges. Grasses indigenous to woodland savannas are shown here, mainly big and little bluestem, Indian grass, switchgrass, and eastern gamma grass. Research indicates that Native Americans were cognizant of the role of fire in keeping the eastern woodlands partially open and grassy.

Parts of southern Missouri—especially the Ozarks with its shallow, rocky soil—have patches of savannas more commonly referred to as glades. These areas of lichen–covered bare rock support distinct, unique suites of plants, reptiles, and birds

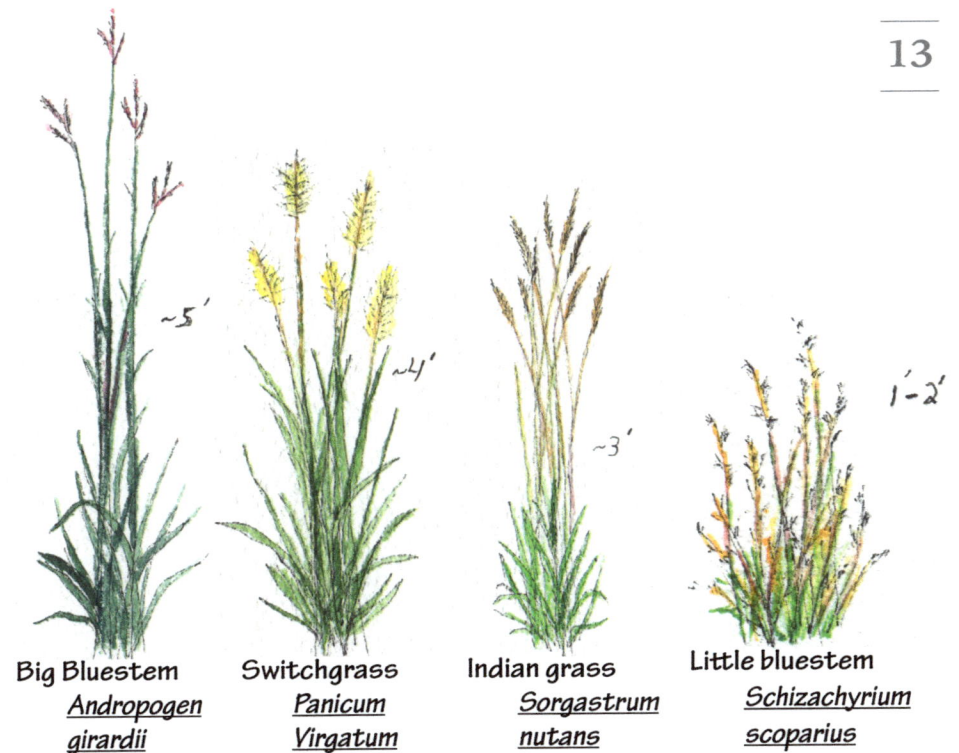

Big Bluestem
Andropogen girardii

Switchgrass
Panicum Virgatum

Indian grass
Sorgastrum nutans

Little bluestem
Schizachyrium scoparius

14

6'-10'

4'-5'

Cordgrass
*Spartinia
pectinata*

Eastern gamma grass
*Tripsicum
dactyloides*

found only in these habitats. They are ecologically fragile areas, sensitive to damage by human foot traffic. Thankfully, the kind of humans most likely to be found there are also a distinct and reclusive group, nature–loving solitary hikers who know where to put their feet.

From the Mississippi Valley into the Great Plains taller grasses are common. Many relatively undisturbed Missouri soils contain a seed bank of native grasses and forbs (broad–leafed herbaceous plants) that need only a good fire to release their dormancy. Big and little bluestem, switchgrass, sideoats grama, and Indian grass are the most common. These were the species the Missouri Department of Conservation was seeking to re–establish in the 1980s, and the ones I learned a whole lot about during a literature survey I conducted for the Missouri Department of Conservation at that time.

While more than thirty inches of rainfall per year will support a forest, ten to thirty inches is perfect for prairie. Farther west the lower rainfall supports fewer and smaller grasses. The suite of native grass species changes, resulting in the so–called short grass prairie, although in many states there is little remaining due to overgrazing.

Bottle Brush
Elmus
nostrix

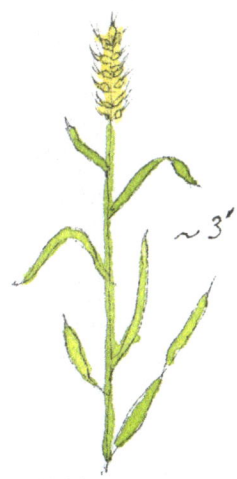

Wild Rye
Elmus
virginicus

Woodland brome
Bromus
pubescens

Sideoats grama
Bouteloa
curtipendula

Sweetgrass
Hierchtoe
oderata

Buffalo grass
Buchloe
dactyloides

Broadleaf
panic grass
Panicum
latifolium

~3'

~3'

~3'

2'-3'

1-2'

1'

1'

Prairie dropseed
Spirobolus
heterolepis

3-4'

16

History and Management

We mostly learn about prairies in history class and are familiar with descriptions of the Great Plains and the vast grasslands that were home to bison and antelope before the settlers came and shot the critters and plowed up the sod. When the drought of the thirties brought the dust bowl years, the grasses were gone. The dust storms blew it away. The rich, deep grassland topsoil, originally ten to thirty feet deep, the product of hundreds of thousands of years of plant growth and decomposition, ended up in adjacent eastern states, even as far away as Washington D.C. Those indigenous grasses, adapted to the climate and the cycles of grazing, were incredible, their seed stalks often taller than a man. There is no telling how many kids wandered off from their wagon trains and were never seen again.

Fires were and still are a natural part of both grassland and forest ecosystems. I have on several occasions taken part in prescribed burns, which practice is now a part of managing both grassland and forest ecosystems. I am hard-put to adequately describe the magnificence of a native grass fire. Unlike the process of burning dead leaves or grass from your yard, grassland fires are raging monsters, with flames leaping to twenty feet in height, the noise a roar like a tornado, and the heat generated is guaranteed to leave nothing living after it passes. Except the grass. As the fire passes over the soil, the crown and roots of the grass are insulated from the fire's heat. After a bit of rain and a little time, the grasses once again shoot up and regrow.

Bison were historically also essential to the grasses' cycles. With hooves comparatively smaller and sharper than domestic livestock, they drove the grass seeds into the soil, where the rain would cover them and facilitate sprouting. The nomadic bison grazed and moved on, leaving behind natural fertilizer. Just imagine all the poop from a herd of thousands of bison. Whew!

Today, the increased interest in preservation of our natural resources has led to collaboration between and among private nonprofits such as the Nature Conservancy, landowners, federal and local government, and conservation groups to reestablish and preserve native grass ecosystems. This effort extends not only to native plants but also to endangered wildlife such as the prairie chicken, ruffed grouse, black–footed ferret, and the American bison.

The Missouri Prairie Foundation is a nonprofit conservation and land trust dedicated to restoring native prairie habitat. It is also home to the Grow Native plant education and marketing program, a valuable resource for landowners seeking to support conservation of native habitats. Northern Boone County, Missouri, where I live, has a natural repository of native grass seeds, including big and little bluestem and Indian grass, evident in pastures, on road banks of rural roads and even along Highway 63. So here's a *BOLO* (Be On The Lookout). Be a grass detective!

Noxious Weeds

Unfortunately for some plants, their lifestyle is not compatible with human activities. The USDA has designated these as noxious weeds. Granted we're talking about a government agency, which operates under the directive to promote and protect the huge industry of American agriculture. And true to the dictates of human progress, we can't let anything interfere with progress. Just ask the Lorax.

One summer of my graduate studies in agronomy, a project found its way to me in the form of a noxious weed survey. I was given a list of plants and my job was to nose around the state and see if I could find any of them. I don't recall all the weed species on the list, but among them was one called fireweed, which is parasitic on the roots of corn in southern states, and an aquatic called *Salvinia molesta* which tends to clog southern waterways and screw up boat navigation.

I was working for the government, with the USDA supporting the project. The Animal and Plant Health Inspection Service (APHIS) and Plant Protection and Quarantine (PPQ) are the agencies which regulate organisms entering the United States across its borders and across state borders. It was actually pretty interesting to learn how this works.

There is a constant influx of shipments that arrive in the US from foreign countries. Some, but not all, arrive at coastal ports where they are subject to inspection. Likewise, some arrive on planes, some are mailed, and some are moved across borders from Canada and Mexico by various and sundry means. I'm not going down that rabbit hole. While wildlife, human, and drug trafficking are all a big deal, it wasn't my concern. What I was looking for were plants that were where they shouldn't be, particularly the ones that were potentially threatening to domestic crops.

Passing inspection, plants may be trucked, flown, or moved by ships to their destination. Some of these plants are not the primary shipment, but are used as packing or piggyback accidentally. Shipments from specific countries are routinely suspect as the source of certain seeds or of disease organisms and therefore are held, quarantined for a time before being sent on. To learn more about this process I was sent to Kansas City to what is known as the Foreign Trade Zone. This is located in a warren of rooms in a complex of limestone caves carved into the

bluffs along the Missouri River north of Kansas City. With their restricted entrance and their natural constant temperature, they are ideal for storage, inspection, and quarantine.

Other repositories of plant material are in the plant collections of colleges and museums. Known as herbaria, the plants are dried specimens, pressed and glued to special sheets of paper, with the date and location of collection, the collector, and the Genus and species of the specimen. I spent many hours and lots of gasoline driving Missouri roads during that hot summer in a car with no air conditioning, window down, and an eight-track tape player blasting out Pure Prairie League and Jim Croce. I visited a number of herbaria, including the one at the Missouri Botanical Gardens in Saint Louis. This awesome collection of plant specimens is housed in a special climate-controlled building open to researchers by appointment only. Imagine the stacks in a huge library where the specimens reside in horizontal cubbyholes in rows of shelves that open on sliding tracks like an accordion. Pretty cool! Just like the archives of the Henry Louis Gates program, *Finding Your Roots* on PBS.

I also spent some time in rail yards, looking for live specimens. Trains moving from state to state tend to pick up windblown plant material and weeds along the way. As trains come into the rail yard and slow prior to uncoupling, the braking process jolts the cars and dislodges seeds which fall off and sprout.

On the Saint Louis trip I needed a knowledgeable botanist who could help me identify the rail yard plants. A helpful person at the herbarium introduced me to an old gentleman named Victor Mulenbach. Not to be confused with the well-known Kansas botanist Victor Moellenbach, my guide was a native Latvian who emigrated to the United States at the time the Soviets took over his country. There he was a noted professor. Here he had to start over at the bottom and work menial jobs until he arrived somehow at the Botanical Gardens as a beloved and respected expert.

On one of those blast furnace days that summer, he accompanied me to the Saint Louis rail yards where we sweated our way up and down the tracks searching for the plants on my list. He taught me several important things that summer. First, to respect the fortitude of the elderly. I was ready for a cold beer while he was still trucking along checking out the plants. Secondly, I learned how to make a peasant hat from a handkerchief to keep the sun from boiling my brains. And last but most important, when I tried to pay him for his help he refused, telling me to repay him by "passing it on," to help another down the line when I had the opportunity. I've never forgotten that humble man or his directive to me.

As with all my stories, I like to pass along some of the humorous aspects of my experiences. One of my discoveries that summer was that *Salvinia molesta* is notoriously difficult to identify. While I was in the Climatron at the Botanical Garden, I noticed a little aquatic floater in one of its pools. As it looked suspiciously like the one on my list, I pointed it out to the person in charge and asked if he could get confirmation of its species, as not all of this genus are pests. It turned out that they could indeed not confirm if it was or wasn't, and as a result they had to clear it out of all their pools. I haven't been back since, as they are probably on the lookout for me and I would end up as the aquatic floater.

Salvinia sp.

D. Canote

The last story has to do with an accidental discovery of a plant that wasn't on my list. As most rural residents know, as a result of early cultivation of hemp as a fiber crop there is a considerable amount of "ditch weed" along the roadsides and waterways of northern Missouri. Any local rural teenager will generally know the location of said plant, although the chances of getting a buzz from it are just about zilch. Still, I was visiting a cousin in Kearney, a little north of Kansas City, on my way home from surveying and he asked me if I wanted to check out the location of a big bunch of the stuff. Evidently there was a lot of local traffic to and from a certain wetland known as Cooley Lake. So off I went, and did I ever find it! The stuff was ten feet tall and thick as a jungle, acres and acres of it thriving in a large wetland. I happened to mention this to my supervisor at the University when I got home and word got around to the powers that be. Long story short, Cooley Lake is no longer a pot haven. I wonder if the law enforcement that did the burning were standing downwind? And if so, how they explained to their families when they went home that night?

Cannabis, sativa

D. Canote

Cooley Lake Conservation Area

Into the Woods

Poems about the woods are among my favorites. "Stopping By Woods on a Snowy Evening" and "The Road Not Taken" evoke thoughts and memories of walking through Missouri woodlands, as well as those of other states I have visited. Even the stories and images of wolves and wicked stepmothers in the books from my childhood never really scared me. The cool greenness in summer, the nostalgia–inducing feeling of autumn woods with their approaching senescence, the silent stark black–and–whiteness of winter, and the excitement of spring wildflowers peeking through the leaf layers humble me with my own insignificance.

Riding horseback down country back roads and through fields, trees offered the contradiction of welcoming shade in the heat of summer combined with the disgust of an equine intent on scraping me off under a tree limb. When I was old enough to climb trees, my mother was both worried about me breaking bones from a fall and aggravated with torn clothing and scraped knees. I recall getting a switching (a slender peach limb on bare legs were the go–to for misbehavior by both Mom and Grandma) for climbing the peach tree in our back yard, not for the danger of it but damage to it, peaches being much desired for both eating and canning.

Both 4–H and church camp, held at Crowder Campgounds in Grand River State Park, were the highlight of my summer vacations. Years later the original scent of Herbal Essence Shampoo would still bring back memories of hikes through those wood. (I lament the loss of its old formula!)

My Hippie House

After spending most of my grad school years in a mobile home park I was pretty tired of city living. When I finally had a job that paid more than a graduate stipend, I decided it was time to look for a real house. My friend Jamin and her then fiance Tim were helping me hunt by keeping an eye on the real estate ads when she came across a photo of a promising rustic cabin. "Oh look, Tim! A hippie house!" She knew what I was looking for and off we went to check it out. I was excited when I saw it, set in the midst of forty acres of mostly woods in southeastern Howard County. A post–and–beam cabin, it had only a wood stove for heat and, lacking water and electricity, wasn't suitable as it was for permanent occupation. But with a little help from some friends I was able to get a construction loan to add on rooms and bring in water and electricity.

I learned a lot from living in that cabin, starting with taking part in a lot of the finishing work and then living a somewhat spartan existence and dealing with the weather and wildlife. Besides the usual furry critters, the site had some things I hadn't previously encountered, namely copperheads and black widow spiders.

In a small site cleared of a few trees to reduce shade, I established a modest garden where I managed to produce enough vegetables to make me happy. I did a lot of my gardening barefoot or in sandals until one day I noticed out of the corner of my eye a movement of a part of the soil and looked down to see a small copperhead about two inches from my foot. Well. I have never been afraid of snakes but I wasn't too excited to see this one so up close and personal. I also respected the snake's right to have a life, so I found an implement and managed to pick it up and carry it into the woods. Thereafter I tended to look before I took a step.

Then one day as I walked out my back door, I noticed an interesting spiderweb in the grooves of the cabin's siding. Always curious about the critters, I looked more closely and saw a shiny black, skinny–legged spider in the web with a large egg case. Whoa, I thought, black widow! They are not particularly rare in Missouri but I had never before seen one alive. I managed to catch her and preserved both spider and egg case in alcohol for my Biology students to see. After that one I encountered several more in storage sheds and learned to check where I put my hands.

At first it was a bit scary living alone there. Daytime I spent walking the woods, locating my boundaries and getting to know the terrain. At night the noises were unfamiliar, and it took me a while to figure out what they all were. I lived in that cabin long enough that eventually I was comfortable enough to walk out into the woods any time of the day or on moonlit nights, along trails I laid out and cleared. The property was at a junction of the northern prairie and the central river valleys of Missouri. At the southernmost terminus of the last Ice Age glacier, there were remnants of the moraine in the form of huge granite boulders and other rocks carried from northern sources, a geologist's dream. The terrain itself was dissected with a couple of small drainages that roared with runoff after a heavy rain. The lower portions of these ephemeral streams with both north and east facing slopes were especially wonderful habitat for many plants not commonly seen. Native orchids, ferns, woodland wildflowers and even golden seal made every walk through the woods an adventure.

It wasn't until I had sold the land and moved (marriage uprooted me again) that I learned of another inhabitant of those woods. My neighbors across the road had two beautiful dogs, boxers, that they housed in a large chain–link pen at night. During the day they had the run of the property but generally stayed near the house. Both the dogs were eventually killed, one in its pen, by what the vet said was a large cat. Another neighbor reported seeing a large, long–tailed cat near dusk crossing the road nearby. These reports coincided with other reports of cougar sightings in nearby areas. I thought about all the times I had walked through those woods, both by day and night, and it dawned on me that cougars hunt from trees.

Into the Garden

Sprouting

There are so many cool songs about the garden. One I first heard at a big gardening convention was written by Greg Brown entitled "Canned Goods" (*One More Goodnight Kiss*, 1988) caught me right in the heart. "...You can taste a little of the summer, Grandma put it all in jars."

It began for me with my Grandma Jesse. Like so many of the other aspects of her life, the garden was a necessary chore if there were going to be victuals for the winter. Although I never heard her say so, I think she loved the ritual of growing and I loved the wonderful taste of fresh produce (well, maybe not the lima beans). Most, if not all country folks we knew spent part of the summer canning. My mom had a big kitchen garden too, and my brothers and I had to do planting and weed duty, and we all three hated it. But that's how you learn, eh?

After I was married, we had a garden where my husband, two daughters and mother–in–law worked every summer. Lillie Irene Blum England was probably more diligent than the rest of

us, and most mornings we would find her out early with her hoe, "…stressing the weeds." I have to digress here a bit and share a special moment in her garden.

We were all doing some weed pulling and the girls, squatting among the radishes, started singing a catchy little song they learned in school about a bed full of ten little bears "…and the little one said 'Roll over, roll over,' and they all rolled over and one fell out, there were nine in bed and the little one said…," sort of the elementary version of "ninety nine bottles of beer" if you will…. Their young voices, perfectly in tune, were one of the sweetest things I have ever heard. It was years later when Angela graduated from high school before I heard them singing together again, harmonizing an Indigo Girls tune, "Closer to Fine." Their voices were still as beautiful as they had been in their grandmother's garden years before.

Through the years I spent in grad school I drifted away from gardening, but learned a lot more about plants. From the chemical and biological process of photosynthesis, the chemical makeup and effects of herbicides and their fate in the environment, to the chemical composition, formation, and contribution of soil properties on plant growth, I was fascinated with the entire process of producing both food and beauty. And after I retired from a career of science teaching and research, I went back to the garden.

Market Gardening

When I finally retired from teaching, I was suffering from withdrawal, feeling I should be getting up at the crack of dawn, rushing off to school to spend the day in intense concentration as surrogate mother, technician, mentor, drill sergeant... whew! So what was I going to do with my time?

The summer before I planned to retire I explored the idea of taking some of my garden's bounty to the local farmers market. I have always been fascinated with the subject of herbs, not so much for their culinary uses but for their therapeutic properties. I decided to concentrate my efforts in how to grow medicinal herbs. The problem was that most market customers weren't very interested in those, they wanted things they could put in their salads, soups, or other dishes. So I worked on growing both. Still, there weren't many market–goers who bought herbs, and I began to expand my sales to other areas.

Since there was only one other vendor at the market selling flowers, I decided to include cut flowers in my sales, along with some of my excess fruits and vegetables. I learned quickly that if you want to be a success in the business, you couldn't grow what everyone else was growing. Along with my buckets of zinnias and sunflowers that people like to use for their own arrangements, I started buying up cute little vases and making my own arrangements and bouquets. Some of what went into these were the foliage and flowers of the larger herbs I grew. That worked. Sales grew.

Then I started experimenting with some other things I didn't see at the market. At one point I had a dozen or more varieties of hot peppers and as many old open–pollinated varieties of heirloom tomatoes. I learned about hoop houses, plastic-covered high tunnels used to extend the growing season. I then bought and constructed a twenty foot by ninety-six foot one, and experimented with types of crops that would otherwise be difficult or impossible to grow in Missouri. Ginger, turmeric and figs were particularly popular, and the Mediterranean–type herbs, like rosemary, lavender, sage, etcetera, loved the heat and humidity of the tunnel.

Eventually other vendors saw what I was doing and began to do the same. The competition began to cut into my sales, and as my body began to complain, I decided it was time to change vocations again. I talked for a couple of years about cutting back before I finally followed up by actually doing it. These days I spend a lot of time reading, painting, and writing, and sewing up useful stuff like aprons, tote bags and in the winter, quilting. And, now that I don't have to rise at the hairy crack of dawn to teach or go to market, I often wake up at five o'clock. But that doesn't keep me from rolling over for a few more hours of sleep.

Chapter Three
Old Stuff

I am quietly amused these days as I scroll through Facebook posts and encounter pictures accompanied by the comment. "How many people have one of these in their home?" or "How many of you have ever used one of these?" or "How many of you even know what this is for?" Invariably, I recognize, own, and even still use the item. So I say to myself, "Am I really that old?" And I guess maybe I am! I mean, I don't feel like I'm that old, or, wait… maybe I do. Darn.

I have the proud distinction of being one of those people born in the aftermath of World War II, a part of the so–called *baby boom*. My family lived in a small town/ rural area of northern Missouri, and many members of our community still used the sort of implements and practiced the sort of subsistence agriculture no longer common today. Butter churns and molds, washboards and wringer washing machines, corn grinders, sprinkling bottles (bottles of water with perforated caps for ironing clothes), and a multitude of other gadgets and devices are now obsolete and "quaint."

I'm thinking these days that maybe it would be good to know about a lot of this stuff, because the news out there is really worrysome. The world is no longer so big, and the distance between us and the rest of the world has shrunk to the time it takes to turn on the news media. As quickly as the pandemic spread, so even more quickly could missiles of global conflict reach our shores.

Watching PBS the other evening it was brought home to me exactly how near our planet is to the literal tipping point of disastrous meltdown. Climate change has progressed to the point that within what is left of my lifetime, I may very will be reverting to using those old–time devices and practices my grandparents used. All the things I bring home from my weekly shopping trips—from food to toilet paper, gasoline to medicine, and a dozen or so library books—may be hard to come by if the global economy goes down the tubes and infrastructure fails.

I can just hear some of you who read this going, "Ffftttt!" Well it's like my Aunt Pauline said so many years ago when I was giving her a pep talk about measures she could take to manage her continual battle with weight gain and her figure. After listening to me prattle on for a minute or two she just turned to me with a smug expression and said, "Just you wait…." Yup, she had the last word.

So here we are back at the old stuff. The old rusty machines, old houses, old practices still have the ability to draw our interest, and I'm not immune to that lure either. It's what made me devote so much time to researching and painting all those bridges in my first book, and what leads me to stop my car as I drive and take photos of all sorts of old houses, machines, and such. Some of these interested me enough to paint them and pass my interest along to you.

The Water Weeder

I don't know if you will ever find an apparatus like this anywhere else in the world. It was featured in a short article in the October 16, 1946 edition of *The Kansas City Star*. A fellow named Forest Gill, a Chillicothe, Missouri duck hunter, owned a forty-acre pond near my home town of Avalon, which was overgrown with waterlilies. It would seem that waterlilies and duck hunting are not compatible, so Mr. Gill designed this device and Avalon residents Harold and Gerald Avery built it for four hundred dollars. The 18 by 5.5 foot boat was powered by a mowing machine motor that also drove a front-mounted sickle bar mower. The mower blade would cut the stems below the water line and the rake teeth cleared away the debris.

Evidently there was not a great demand for the water weeder, even though it would appear to be a work of entrepreneurial genius. From the picture it looks like the weeder at least provided a way to pass a nice summer afternoon with the kids.

Old Highway Maintainer

I would like to start this essay with a brief diversion to explain how I came to do the painting. During my teaching career I was always looking for opportunities to expand my teaching repertoire of science expertise. One summer I traveled to Albuquerque, New Mexico for a week–long course in Materials Science. This discipline is designed for students who don't want to take the college route but might be interested in careers in industry. I hoped to talk our school district into adding Materials Science to the curriculum.

Google defines Materials Science as "an interdisciplinary field concerned with the understanding and application of the properties of matter." The solid material that makes up the non–biological infrastructure of our modern world consists primarily of metals, ceramics, polymers, semiconductors, and composites. Look around you and think about all the nonliving things you see and consider how they are made—from ink pens to highways, computers, cell phones, homes and office buildings, motor vehicles, and appliances—all composed of materials.

Getting back to my camp experience, I was immersed for a week with a group of about two dozen other teachers in lab experiments and field trips to become acquainted with the basics of materials. On a field trip to Rio Grand Jewelry we saw the process of making what are referred to as "findings," the materials that make up settings, supports, and chains for gem stones. Another trip took us into the desert to an iron–works foundry where we watched the blacksmithing of wrought iron.

Having set the scene of this trip, we finally get to the subject of my painting. As we drove along the desert road to the foundry, I looked out the bus window and saw an old piece of rusty machinery sitting by the wayside, and on the way back from our visit was able to get a photo. It was a very old version of the road maintainer, a vehicle used to smooth and shape the surface of rural dirt and gravel roads.

Some research helped me identify it as a vintage steam–driven model produced by J.D. Adams Manufacturing Company. The first model, invented in 1885, was horse– or mule–drawn, referred to as a leaning pull grader, made in Indianapolis, Indiana. A #10 model was made in 1928, later redesigned in 1935 with a side–wards leaning blade to direct graded material to the side. This WWII version was probably the model I had photographed, having survived so long only due to the dry desert conditions.

The road maintainer, or road grader as we referred to it, is a part of my childhood memories walking and riding on horseback and old pickups along our rural roads. If I wasn't in a direct encounter—avoiding having to meet or follow one as it chugged along a narrow road—it was listening to the residents as they came into the Post Office where my mom was postmaster. Generally they were complaining about the road being too flat so that rainwater cut ruts that wouldn't drain, or that all the gravel was pushed off the road bed into the ditch or was left in a ridge down the middle, or some other generally aggravating scenario. Of course, if it didn't get graded in a timely fashion they complained about that too. But for many years there was no money in the county budget to pay for an operator, so it all depended on volunteer labor, as shown in this newspaper clipping from 1891.

The Avalon Aurora says a number of south side farmers have agreed to give one day each with teams to work the road grader on the bottom roads leading from Avalon to Chillicothe. Hurrah for those enterprising farmers. May their numbers increase.

Personally I tried to avoid horseback riding anywhere the grader was working. Horses, regardless of how well broke they are, don't like noisy machinery and will either start bucking or turn tail and run the other way, or both, giving very little heed to the rider's efforts at control. And it is totally disgusting and humiliating when you have to pick yourself up out of the ditch and limp several miles back home.

Old Hay Days

The hay barn in this painting was done from a black and white photo sent to me by one of my cousins, Loyd Canning. When he and his wife, Judy, first moved to their farm near Kearney, Missouri, they were still in farming mode, putting up hay the old way and loading the loose hay into the barn loft. At that time they were using an old John Deere tractor, but for my painting I decided to take artistic license and replaced the tractor with a team of horses.

Today, one rarely sees loose hay being harvested unless you drive through Amish country. Hay is baled in the field, loaded or 'bucked' onto a flatbed wagon (square bales) and hauled to a barn for storage, or into large round bales which are wrapped in netting and moved from the field and aligned in rows at another location. Some big bales may be wrapped in a plastic cover rather than netting which encourages the hay to ferment to a condition referred to as silage.

Many if not most of you who read this are likely not country folks, but there are some current situations that may bring home to you the relevance of hay to modern events. If you consume meat, especially beef, you may logically infer that cows eat grass and grass gets made into hay. But if you follow the news you know there is a campaign to cut the cows out of

the human food chain because cattle are a huge producer of methane, a notorious greenhouse gas. So if the cattle go, then so will the hay. But hey... so back to the hay tales.

Making Hay While the Sun Shines

I maybe should insert a little information here, for those who are not familiar with farming. And if you aren't into farming info you might just want to skip this part. The teacher in me can't help it. Making hay starts with mowing. Unlike mowing grass to just cut it short, grasses and other forbs (nongrasses) for hay must be cut neatly at the base into long stems, which is done with what is called a sickle bar mower. The small triangular blades oscillate back and forth laterally and have to be regularly replaced as they break or break loose when they meet with particularly dry hard weed stems. This is part of the fun of putting up hay. I didn't have to do this, but I know how much fun it was because I got to listen to a blistering running commentary while then–husband David got the mower ready.

After mowing, the hay is allowed to lay for a day or two to dry, and then raked with a tractor–drawn side delivery rake into long bundles called windrows. Then the baler moves along the windrow, feeding the dry hay into the baler where it is rolled or packed into compact bales and wrapped with netting or tied with wire or twine. Rectangular, also known as "square" bales, are loaded onto a wagon or truck and hauled to the barn where they are thrown, lifted, or moved by elevator to an upper level or "loft" for storage.

One final note for the aspiring hay entrepreneur, if baled too green, i.e. not thoroughly dried in the field, the hay will begin to compost, a process that generates a tremendous amount of heat. Bales have been know to spontaneously combust—on the field, stacked on the wagon going down the road, or even after the bales are stacked into the hay loft. And then, "...it's a hot time in the old town tonight," hey, hey, hay!

My Hay Days

As a girl growing up in a small town, all my exposure to hay was second hand. On Halloween one of the local farmers would hitch up a flat–bed wagon, line up some straw or hay bales around the edge and load up a bunch of us kids for a hay ride. He would haul us up and down the roads for an hour or two, the riders carrying on, singing, (maybe some canoodling if it was after dark), and we would end up at a bonfire for some roasted hot dogs and marshmallows. As the old folks used to say when something was particularly wondrous or they were having fun (or maybe not), "Boy, howdy!"

When the teenage years hit, us girls would volunteer for iced tea and lemonade duty when the boys were putting up hay. They would come in all sweaty, tan bared chests glistening and covered with bits of hay, pour a dipper of water from the well pump over their heads and then shake like dogs, sending us squealing and giggling in all directions. Boy, howdy! Well, the hay romance faded away, as all those old rosy memories are wont to do. Later encounters with hay were not so rosy.

When I first married and moved to the farm with my husband, we had a small herd of beef cattle and had enough pasture that we decided to bale some hay for winter. David did the mowing and I had the relatively easy job of driving the tractor to rake the dry hay into windrows. To do this, I would start raking longways along the field, turn at the end of the field and rake back along the same row, throwing the hay into the first pile to make a thicker windrow layer to bale. The hazardous part of raking is that as the rake scrapes the ground on the first pass up the row it stirs up resident colonies of ground–nesting bumblebees. Then when you come back for the second pass with the rake, the are waiting for you and you have to drive through any angry mob of ticked off black and yellow bombs. Not fun.

When we first decided to put up hay we became the proud owners of an Allis–Chalmers round baler. This device from hell, when it was working, would spit out small round bales of variable size and shape, with intermittent and variable periods of breakdown and repair. Quite often this would come at the end of a long, hot, sweaty day as we were trying to get the last windrow baled. As a rule, as the sun drops toward the western horizon, the temperature drops and the ground cools. At the same time, the moisture in the air above the ground condenses and settles into the formerly dry hay. That's when the devil moves into the baler, and we learned to just leave the @#&%*! baler in the field and go to the house.

Kimchee for Cows

It may surprise you the know that baling hay is not the only thing you can do with cut grasses. Cattle have for many years—decades if not centuries—enjoyed the culinary and health benefits of fermented plant foods. When raw grasses are enclosed in oxygen–deprived environments they undergo the same process of acid anaerobic fermentation, similar to the process of producing sauerkraut or kimchee. This process enhances the nutritional benefits of the plant material and allows it to be stored in a stable form until it is consumed. The fermented plant material is called ensilage or silage for short.

The tall cylindrical farm towers used to store silage are called silos, and were once a common sight among most farm buildings. On modern farms the silo has been replaced with tarp–covered concrete pits, open on one side for access for filling and removing the finished silage. And like sauerkraut and kimchee, the fermented product is highly odoriferous, i.e. stinky, only more so. Imagine the smell of a garage–sized pit of bad sauerkraut! Boy, howdy!

The Sorghum Press

A favorite among the many media postings I see these days are those from the Facebook group, "Avalon Then and Now." Many of my home town friends and acquaintances are gone, or scattered far and wide, but there is still a core of loyal Avalonians who have memories (fond or otherwise) of the lives of our forefathers and mothers.

The old ways, those of the previous century, were well documented after personal cameras became widely available and affordable. These days, as we old folks start cleaning out a life's worth of detritus from our shelves and attics we unearth a wealth of old photos and articles from our private archives. A couple of these I ran across documented the process of making sorghum molasses.

Molasses 101

Molasses may be made from the juices of a variety of plants, but most commonly from either sugar cane or grain sorghum. The history of molasses making is documented to 500 B.C.E. in India. Brought to the Americas by early explorers, it was an integral part of the slave trade as a raw material in production of rum. Initially it was probably made from sugar cane, as sugar was also a desirable product.

Molasses–Making the Country Way

Corn, sugar cane, and grain sorghum are closely related members of the grass family, all of which thrive in temperate and tropical conditions. All these plants convert the glucose from photosynthesis to sucrose and store it temporarily in the stem or "cane." Molasses is made from sweet sorghum varieties which have particularly high sugar content.

At the peak of its growth, the sorghum cane is cut, the leaves removed, and the juices are squeezed out using a roller mill. Stalks are fed, one at a time, between the rollers and the juice is collected in buckets under the mill. Juice is finally squeezed through cloth bags to filter out debris.

The heavy dark molasses syrup is the result of one or more cycles of refining. The process of boiling the juice to evaporate the water is done in large, shallow boiler pans approximately seven

feet long by three feet wide by twelve inches deep, as shown in this painting. The pan is situated on top of an elongated wood–fired oven, kept at a boil for six to seven hours, with continuous stirring and skimming to remove cane residue. Logs for the fire are the length of the oven to maintain an even heat. Finally the thickened liquid is cooled, precipitating the sugar crystals which are separated out leaving molasses syrup.

Between stirring the molasses and feeding logs into the oven, the process is hugely labor intensive. It just wears me out to think about it.

The Final Product

In commercial production, mechanization has taken the place of the laborious method previously described. The product of a single cycle of refinement is light molasses, used for flavoring in cooking. Dark molasses is obtained after a second cycle of refining and has a stronger, richer flavor. A final cycle yields blackstrap molasses, a tarry viscous syrup with enhanced health benefits as it has a higher vitamin and mineral content of calcium, magnesium, potassium, and iron.

Molasses is somewhat of an acquired taste, perhaps most appreciated by an older generation who used it in place of refined white sugar during periods of wartime rationing. It is used today in baking, adding a rich earthy flavor to cakes and cookies.

There are also other uses for molasses, and for the sorghum plant other than for molasses. As a chelating agent, molasses binds with metals and is used for rust removal and soil amendments. Added to livestock feed, it increases the palatability and nutrition of these sweet feed mixes. In the mid–western states and Great Plains, where limited rainfall and high temperatures limit corn production, sorghum has also been grown for forage and silage. Certain varieties are considered more suitable than corn for ethanol production.

In olden days making sorghum was an occasion for a community gathering. Not every family had a cane press or mule, so a whole passel of folks would gather to help, bringing food and fiddles for a party. In case you are interested in folk music, here are a few lines from an old song recorded by folk singer Art Thieme on his album *The Older I Get, the Better I Was*, referencing sorghum making. I have set the chorus down as I learned it, because traditional songs allow that liberty.

"Bye And Bye"

Well the time of the year that I like the best
Is the time when the mule walks 'round the press
Girls put on their gingham dress
Bye an' bye an' bye an' bye

Well the leaves get red and the ground gets cold
Sap's gonna rise so I've been told
I don't care if the frost is comin'
Bye an' bye an' bye an' bye

Well, to add incentive there may also have been a little additional juice supplied.

This house, lost somewhere in the countryside of north Missouri, was the home of my paternal great-grandparents, William Wilie and Lydia Catherine (Nau) Deardorff. There is nothing eerie about the old house. It owes its place in this writing to the style and detail of its construction along with its place in my family history. I bear this grandmother's middle name.

Chapter Four
Old, Eerie, and Interesting Buildings

About the time I started my first book, I began to look at the world differently. It started with my painting. As I looked through photographs for painting subjects, I realized that something about their composition just wasn't very interesting. That made me change the way I took photos, made me think about the angle and perspective, what to leave out and what to emphasize.

Then in my research on bridges I also began to pay more attention to buildings and architecture and to suspect that maybe there was a frustrated engineer hiding in me, finally creeping out. Or maybe it was just an excuse to paint buildings, for the challenge of it.

Things that are different from the norm tend to draw my eye, and if they are unusually different will call for a second look. As a painter I am an admitted realist, so the more detail I notice in a scene or an object the more it interests me. Up to a point— I'm not a masochist.

I also like quirky subjects, things that sometimes cause people to look at me a bit strangely. That makes me smile. And finally, I am intrigued by the borderline occult although I haven't made up my mind about ghosts, and prefer to leave that decision for much, much later.

Churches

Somewhere along the line I lost my church–going habit. I can't say it was because I lost my faith, although the structure of my spirituality did undergo a renovation as I revealed in my essay "Mother Earth." I found my beliefs becoming increasingly amorphous, but still with remnants of my Protestant Presbyterian upbringing.

Through the years, though, I have nearly always had the same reaction when I enter an empty church. Like old schools and public buildings, with years of occupation churches seem to become imbued with the spiritual outpouring of the people who come to worship. There is almost, just at the edge of hearing, a faint whispering of voices, an echo of songs, an ephemeral something that brushes the skin like a memory.

I'm not in churches much these days, but I love to slow down as I drive past them. A lot of the old country churches are still standing. Those that haven't been replaced by more modern buildings are the most interesting to me, especially the ones that need a little TLC. I get the feeling that there would be a slotted board prominent on the wall listing the numbers of the hymns for the day's service, and the seating would probably be the un-padded pews of my childhood.

Unfortunately, as the small towns across the country lose their population to larger towns and cities with more attractive amenities and job opportunities, so do the churches lose their congregations. Our lives are so mobile. Changing jobs and even professions, often people don't stay long enough in one home, one community, one state, or even one country to put down real roots and get to know one another. And with the dwindling church body, the community loses a vital lynch pin that provides the "tie that binds" and perhaps the moral glue that was the inheritance from our country's founding fathers.

Whether we worship in the temple, the mosque, the synagogue, or the cathedral, whether the congregation is that of a small-town or rural country church or one of hundreds or thousands, the shared spiritual experience would seem to me to tap into the human consciousness to bring us closer together. As a people, a nation, and a global body, this is a time in the history of our species that we sorely need.

Saint Vincent de Paul Cathedral, Kansas City, Missouri

A year or so ago I had the opportunity to reconnect with cousins from my dad's side of the family. Ya gotta love Facebook. Although I silently curse it when I'm still sitting at the computer at midnight, mindlessly scrolling on and on—through the food recipes that make me drool, the endlessly entertaining pet tricks and kid mishaps, the political propaganda (skip that), sartorial ads, and religious

beseechments—I could go on and on but you get the idea. I'll bet you even do it yourself. What I really look for is the postings with pictures of friends and family, but it just sucks me in.

So one day I ran across a posting with the last name of some cousins I had been out of touch with for many years, and we ended up connecting eventually on the telephone. They were doing family tree searches and wanted to pick my brain about my records and photos. It had been probably fifty years since I last saw and talked with them. To my delight and amazement my cousin Frances, affectionately known as Pud (short for Puddin') to all the family, was still alive and well at eighty–nine. Her daughter and I spent an hour or so on the phone catching up.

In spite of my misgivings, pandemic or not, we made arrangements to meet and I drove one Sunday to Pleasant Hill, Missouri where Kathy Bruno, one of Pud's daughters, lives.

Three of the daughters, Kathy, Mary Frances (named after my mother), and Opal (named after her grandmother), were able to get together that day. Kathy's husband Ron drove us into Kansas City to pick up Pud. She was still working a few hours a week in the bookstore at St. Vincent de Paul Academy, downtown on Flora Avenue. As we drove into the parking lot, I looked up at the cathedral adjacent to the Academy building and saw a subject to paint.

St. Vincent de Paul Cathedral is a magnificent example of architecture which originated in northern France during the twelfth century CE. Developed from Norman designs, the Gothic style is distinguished by three main characteristics. If you have occasion to visit this church or a similar large cathedral, you might see if you can recognize these features.

Most visible of these features is the pointed or ogival arch, as opposed to the rounded arch seen in the construction of Roman bridges, aqueducts and buildings. This arch design appeared in India as early as the eighth century B.C.E. where it was used to span passageways. In Gothic cathedrals it is visible in the shapes of the windows, and here in Missouri it is even seen in smaller Protestant churches.

Secondly, the construction of keeps and castles, whose buildings and walls featured large rooms, led to pointed rib vaults above the interior, appearing as a series of large four-legged spiders, each with a central keystone connecting the ribs.

Finally, as the design evolved, the increasing weight of walls and ceilings called for reinforcement to prevent collapse of the walls. Buttresses were added to the exterior as braces that kept the walls from bowing outward.

A PBS special documented both the fire and the original construction of the cathedral of Notre Dame de Paris, which included details of Gothic construction. If at some point you are able to view this special, it is riveting. A second more recent documentary records the process of reconstruction of the cathedral. It is serendipitous that so often when I am researching a topic it begins to show up everywhere.

Close Encounters

First Encounter

Have you ever visited an old empty building? Especially in the evening? It's as if, as you stand there in an abandoned hallway or room there are echoes, almost heard but not very substantial, voices, doors opening, doors closing, footsteps, something unseen but just around a corner, down a passageway. I can't say I've ever encountered a ghost, but I have had some interesting experiences that made me wonder.

When I was younger, perhaps middle school or high school age, my aunts and uncles from my father's family visited for a weekend, and we went off on one of their drive–arounds, looking at old houses, cemeteries, places from their earlier years. There was only one cousin, Pud, older and otherwise occupied, on that side of the family and she rarely came along on those visits, so I was usually the only non–adult present. That meant as long as I kept my mouth shut I got to do a lot of listening in as they proceeded to basically forget I was there. There isn't much of that around these days, since (sadly, in my opinion) most kids aren't taught they are to be seen and not heard. There were no cell phones at that time, game gizmos, or other things to distract, and as I didn't have a lot of cohorts growing up in a small town I spent more time around the "old folks" (anyone over thirty) and was used to grown–up conversation.

On one occasion we were revisiting the old home site in a remote rural location near Hale, Missouri, of some relative extinct by quite a few years. Long abandoned, the house was empty of all but a few pieces of broken furniture—chairs, a desk, a table—and a lot of dust and cobwebs. There used to be a lot of such old houses around, especially in the country near rural towns where the turnover of real estate is generally slow. It's possible there had been no one at all in the house since it was last occupants moved or passed on, no one to inherit or who cared what happened to it, and the creaks and groans often heard in heated and occupied buildings had long since moved on to more interesting places.

As we moved through the rooms I found myself alone in what had probably been a "sitting room," where an old desk resided in a corner, with dusty cubbyholes and half–open drawers. Of course I was drawn to it to see if anything was left behind.

Sure enough, I unearthed a small stationery tablet, probably about six by eight inches, such as people used to use to write letters. However, in this one someone had copied a poem, a fairly long one, and as I read it I felt as though the writer had left behind a memory of his or her own life. I took it home and read and re–read it until I had memorized some thirty verses. In those years I was gifted with the ability to memorize easily, and I still use that poem to put myself to sleep some nights. I later came across the poem in a collection and learned its title,

*I am indebted to my friend, Nile Kemble for his photo of this old abandoned
house in eastern Nebraska, no doubt haunted by ghosts of its own.*

"Locksley Hall" by Alfred Lord Tennyson. Written in 1835, in many ways it is prophetic in foreseeing developments in aviation and commerce, but mainly it is a story of unrequited love, so of course it appealed to an impressionable young mind. The memory of the day, the old house, and the lasting impression of the poem can still bring a slight chill to my mind, a haunting without the ghost.

Second Encounter

This story will take a bit of introduction, a preface to where I was and why, so be patient as you read and I'll get to the point in a bit.

I graduated from high school in 1964 and dutifully left for college when my mother insisted, "You will become a teacher." I was actually following in her footsteps, attending the same college, then Northwest Missouri State, now part of the University system. Originally founded as a teachers college (normal school), and part of the state's teachers college collection, it started me on the requisite courses toward graduation.

Thanks to the National Defense Student Loan Program my tuition, books, and room and board were paid for, but anything extra had to come out of my pocket. Mom sent me a small check occasionally, but I supplemented that by working at the front desk of my dorm. In those days the dorms were not coed.

Male visitors had to sign in (only to the lounge) and residents had to sign out after six p.m. with a curfew of ten p.m. That provided enough money for an occasional pizza (onion, which was the cheapest), but not much else. A friend who I dated for a bit worked doing yard work and odd jobs for a music professor, Miss Ruth Miller, at the on–campus elementary school, and he was able to get me a job doing housecleaning for her once a week.

As I walked to and from Miss Miller's house, I passed near a stable. Did I tell you I was a horse–crazy girl? So of course I had to sort of "drop in" to breathe in the lovely scent of hay, horse manure, and saddle soap. I made friends with the stable manager who understood my weakness and indulged visits.

One evening as I walked back to the dorm I stopped in to visit the barn, where no horses were then in residence and no one was around to say I couldn't. I can recall vividly as I stepped into the barn, rays of the setting sun shone through a window at the west end of the stable opposite the door. The warm glow of evening light reflected off particles of dust in the air and, as I inhaled the scents of hay, horse and barn, I began to hear soft muted sounds. The stomp of hooves, snorts, rustles of hay and clink of harness—bits and buckles—gave me an eerie sensation as the hair rose on the back of my neck. I had never encountered the sensation before and, feeling like I had walked into a ghost story, proceeded to back out the door. Were there ghosts there, or was it my imagination?

D Canote

Echoes

It has been my experience that buildings still in use, particularly old ones, may at times give a sense of prescience, especially at night after everyone has gone home. During my first years of teaching, my then–husband David and I taught at the same school in Malta Bend, Missouri. Teachers of course are always enlisted into secondary duties such as class or club sponsor, athletic events and so forth, which meant we were often in the building for after–school activities. Occasionally we were the last ones out and would be required to turn off lights and close the building for the night. At these times one could hear the strangest sounds, muffled creaks, groans and whispers, likely a response to changes in temperature or infrastructure systems doing their job. Still, it was sometimes unnerving and we would reflect on it with comments about the supernatural. His theory, which actually appealed to me, was that during the day the building absorbed the sounds of its occupation and at night, after everyone had gone home, the sounds would come back out of the walls.

The painting that accompanies this essay is of an old abandoned building in Bland, Missouri. I was passing through the small town on my way home from a road trip and, always on the lookout for possible subjects to paint, took a couple of quick shots. The large old building was obviously long unused, with some windows boarded up and the grounds mostly uncared for. Later, I talked with a friend, Bruce Sassman, who lived in Bland to find out some history of the building. It was obviously not a house but instead designed to house offices or apartments. Located across the street from a large industrial building, originally a broom factory and later home to the D. E. Brown Shoe Company, Bruce said it was an apartment building and served as a residence for factory workers.

While the building appears structurally sound, only a few years without occupants will often result in deterioration on the inside of a building. Like the human mind, regardless of external appearance, if there is no one home there is a sadness about an empty building. Memories of all the events and lives that were once housed in the structure itself are lost, only echoes are left. Like the words from a Kansas song by Kerry Livgren, "…All we are is dust in the wind."

The Outhouse

As already noted, kids these days—anyone under the age of fifty—think it is nifty to rediscover old things, including obscure household and farm items, quaint places and names, and even old people. At some point it occurred to me that there is an item going the way of the Model T that is no longer in wide-spread use that could stand to be rediscovered. So I'm going to pass along some information on the outhouse.

I decided to search online for some history and general information. What I didn't expect was the wealth of references and the breadth of coverage on the topic. Well, who 'da thunk it? I was amazed at the apparent fascination with the topic. Evidently the business of doing one's business was at one time big business! What a hoot!

For those of you who have never used an outhouse or have limited knowledge about them, I'll fill you in on some history and relevant trivia that you can use on the next social occasion when there is a lull in the conversation.

The History of the Outhouse

While the history of providing for bodily functions is extensive, I don't plan to write a whole lot on this topic. I will refer you to a couple of internet sources that have some interesting information. Sue Bowman, Southeast Pennsylvania correspondent for *Cappers Farmer*, provided a Nov 12, 2015 article entitled "Pondering the Privy: A History of Outhouses" which gives a pretty extensive review. The site homestead.org also has a great resource entitled "The Poo Papers" (LOL) that has some great photos.

Before the innovation of a municipal water supply and indoor plumbing, taking care of one's business had to be provided for in a more dignified fashion than the proverbial cub bear method. Where possible, especially in larger towns and cities, a small separate building was erected behind the residence and far enough away so as to not be an olfactory offense. Referred to as the outhouse, privy, loo, or other less delicate names, and depending on the number of individuals to be accommodated, the facility was generally one small room just large enough to contain a short bench with one or two holes of a size to fit the standard bottom. In prolific families with lots of small bottoms, one or more smaller holes might be provided. In the era of early inns and boarding houses privies might have separate facilities for the ladies and gents, or might even be multistory. Now that provides for some interesting logistical speculations, eh?

Before the outhouse was erected, a trench or pit called a cess-pit was dug deep enough to last for a considerable time.

Excavations of historical sites reveal that these pits were also a repository for disposal of broken bottles, dishes, clothing, spent ammunition, and other items characteristic of the period of occupation. It was also common for the privy to be provided with a bucket or bin containing quicklime (calcium oxide or CaO) that was sprinkled into the pit periodically to hasten decomposition and reduce odor. And finally, prior to the invention of toilet tissue when some alternative 'wiper' was needed, softened paper, corn cobs, and the like were provided.

Painting My First Outhouse

Driving along a Missouri blacktop road, I passed an old outhouse in the woods near Baldwin School, a well–preserved country schoolhouse on Route A in Howard County. Thinking it would make a nice woodland scene, I took a photo. This was the standard, old–time privy, weathered and doubtless recalled fondly by many bottoms. I later gifted the painting to a quirky teacher friend, Paul Scoville, at his retirement party and had to paint it a second time. (I knew he would appreciate the thoughtfulness of the subject, a corollary to a bad day in the classroom.)

The Old Avalon Outhouse

During a recent visit to my old hometown for the now annual Memorial Day Avalon reunion, we were reminiscing about old pictures and buildings that were now gone, when one of the townies mentioned that one of the two outhouses from the old school was still standing. Built of the ubiquitous large red bricks, with some re–mortaring and patching, the boy's john still sat next to the street on the west side of the schoolhouse lot. I took a photo of it thinking it might make a good painting.

There was a lot of nostalgia passed around about those days, names of people long gone, where they lived and what shenanigans they got up to, and evidence of a lot of warm and fuzzy feelings about preserving what is left. The last discussion before I left to come home was that the old outhouse might be refurbished and a sign set next to it—Avalon Rest Stop.

Other Outhouses I Have Known

My first recollections of the outhouse were from the years at my Grandma Jesse's place. Due to occasional family problems, it was not unusual for family members to be relieved of their parental duties as they dealt with loss of a spouse, illnesses, or other issues. At those times Grandma was the designated guardian, so my brothers and I, as well as various cousins, were periodically consigned to her custody.

Like many rural homes in those years, her house had no indoor plumbing, so we were well acquainted with the outdoor sanitation facility. Her outhouse was not free–standing as most were, but was attached to the east side of the chicken house and accessed by a sidewalk through the chicken yard. The only problem with that was in those years Grandma had a big red rooster. (But that was before I stayed with her.) Mostly it was a problem for my brother Jerry who was terrorized by it and as a result suffered occasional episodes of constipation as he would put off his business as long as possible. After "disappearing" the rooster (refer to an earlier story in my first book) the rooster was no longer a problem.

However, there were some issues that made me anxious during my childhood. Most of these were in the realm of small six– or eight–legged creatures. Wasps were and still are a nuisance in outdoor buildings and my worst fears were not only about being stung, but about where I would be stung!

Then there was the issue before toilet tissue of a suitable material to serve that purpose. The solution for most families, including ours, was Sears Roebuck and Montgomery Ward catalogs. As for many rural homes in those days, most of our shopping was done by mail order, so there was always a ready supply of last year's catalog issue, about two inches thick, that was hung over a piece of string on the outhouse wall. The black and white pages were better than the color pages because they were thinner and could be held between two hands and scrubbed together to soften the sheet. I know that technique endures in the memories of even the writers of TV scripts. I was watching a rerun of *Matlock* recently and, having endured the continued frustrating requests of a full house of unwanted guests, and being accosted with one whining fellow complaining that the bathroom was out of toilet paper, Matlock grabbed up the closest newspaper, furiously scrubbing it between his fists, and wordlessly thrust it into the hands of the unfortunate puzzled guest.

On one childhood visit to Grandma's outhouse I was sitting there, having taken care of my business, and lifted the pages of the catalog to tear out what I wanted, where to my horror I found myself staring into the multiple shining eyes of a very large, hairy wolf spider which was spread out across the inside. If I hadn't been finished before, I was then. I expect Grandma heard me scream all the way to the house. Thereafter I always gave the catalog a good whack when I went in, to make sure there were no surprises.

The last outhouse I had occasion to use was in 1994, when I bought the cabin and forty acres of woods in Howard County, Missouri. The cabin, my "hippy house," built by its former owners as a getaway from town. The cabin had no water, hence no bathroom, so I had to do some remodeling before I could use it as a permanent residence. But there was an outhouse there, and an elegant one it was, with an Anderson window and wallpapered with cover pages from the Smithsonian magazine. It was a one–holer with a regular toilet seat and hinged lid

fastened to the bench. The window was on the south or right–hand wall as you were seated and gave a beautiful view of the surrounding woods. I did a bit of meaningful reflection there in the weeks it took to get a water supply to the house and the necessary work done for indoor plumbing. The toilet paper was confined in a gallon plastic coffee can and I never encountered any surprises in the toilet paper roll.

The Plein Aire Privy

A few other encounters with alternative potties come to mind before I close out this fascinating topic (snicker, snicker).

More appropriate to painting, the term plein aire refers to out–doors. Inevitably, one may feel the call of nature when no secluded facilities are available. I have, on a couple of occasions, encountered some unique alternatives to the outhouse. One winter a visit to a friend in northern Minnesota included a midnight dogsled ride behind a team of malamutes (boy those big dogs sure stink). The next evening we camped overnight in a primitive cabin in the woods. When I asked directions to the facilities I was shown a path into the woods. A short walk led to a clearing, in the middle of which sat a solitary camping toilet. There it sat (I sat) amidst the splendor of the winter snow, undoubtedly the most sublime rest stop of my life.

One final, unique facility I ran across sat at the intersection of two rural roads in Hauchita, New Mexico. I'm not sure how often it was used, but it sure was cute!

Chapter Five
Cradle to Grave

I wondered to myself, how does one go about describing a lifetime of experiences? Once again I thought about Forrest Gump's mother and her box of chocolates. It so happens that is how this book came about—I never knew where I was going or what would turn out when I started. While the stories pretty much meander back and forth from my childhood to the present, putting them all together in some coherent manner was a huge challenge. While I wouldn't want my reader to be bored by predictability, I also hope to finish in a way that ties these last essays together.

I am also using this chapter as a vehicle to include some poetry. I haven't written poetry for many years. Nearly all of my collection, perhaps fifty or so total, were from my so-called middle years of graduate school. I was always drawn to the meter and rhyme of the older style of poems, but Sandburg and similar poets also drew me with their animate/inanimate similes—"the fog comes on little cat feet" and "hog farmer, butcher to the world"—wonderful phrases that evoke instant images, an alternate way of seeing!

If I were to write poetry these days they would contain less angst, less anger, less sorrow. The years have a way of smoothing away edges, soothing most if not all the wounds, and giving a perspective only earned with age and experience. Those I have chosen to share here are a small sampling from a previous life.

What fools are those
Who seek to know
But knowing,
Never seek to grow.

Who die alone
And never learn
There's no deposit,
No return.

Life

This is a really hard topic to write about, not because I dread the alternative, but because there are so many aspects of life to consider.

The Living Condition

So what is life? First of all, let me say "Yaaaaay Life!" I'm all for it, especially for me, my family, my friends, and all the good, generous, caring, creative, positive people world wide. Cruel, selfish, greedy, nasty–tempered, destructive and likewise negative people, not so much. In spite of the right–to–life folks, it might benefit the human condition if certain individuals weren't born. Such a terrible, un–Christian attitude, Dorothy. After all, were it not for the fact that your mother was unable to access the single bathroom in the hall at the end of the floor in our apartment building in Chicago in 1945, you wouldn't be here either! Shame on you!

And anyway, who cares what I think. And what do I care what they think. And in case you are one of these people who read with a corrective red pen in hand, those are declarative sentences, not interrogative.

The freedom of hours and days in the outdoors as a child allowed me to observe and interact intimately with life. Bugs, spiders, frogs, and worms were the most interesting because they were small and easy for me to detain long enough to satisfy my curiosity. Thus began my vocation as a naturalist, and to a career as a biology teacher.

Life Cycles

The first introduction I had to life cycles was probably something about butterflies. Think about it. Don't most kids encounter butterflies and doesn't it inspire interest and wonder to think about the beauty and freedom of being able to live like that? Imagine taking to the air on a sunny day and just wafting about, any way the wind blows, looking for a flower—tra la la la. So that's a good way to start teaching a child about nature. Birth, growth and change, and then the natural outcome of life. Not so close to personal but a little introduction to the sadness that creatures don't live forever.

As any artist will tell you, it takes a bit of distance to gain perspective and to see or intuit where things begin and end. A younger person reading this possibly won't appreciate that fact. It's easy for humans to understand life cycles from the perspective of a butterfly, or even a small furry critter like a pet, whose life cycles we can watch play out many times over the course of our lives; more difficult when the life cycle is our own.

Life cycle of an insect

OBSERVATIONS ON AQUATIC CRITTERS

Exchanging end-for–end and up for down,
Each larval thread pursues its frantic quest
For meaning in its four–dimensional existence
Having little congress with its fellow or with me.
I see some similarity between its to–and–froing
And my own disorganized existence.

Perhaps we all are larval forms
Of some exquisite frail and transitory flight
Metamorphosing and cracking open shells,
Emerging from incompleteness to readiness,
Mating, begetting, and leaving behind
Both discarded juvenile ghosts and new potential.

Life Lessons

I vaguely remember being young—no wait—I remember it very well, because I had a glorious youth. After my father died of lung cancer in 1949, life was lean for a while. My mother, two brothers, and I depended on the support of family and neighbors to feed and clothe ourselves. But in spite of the hard economic conditions of the late 1940s and 50s, I don't recall ever feeling that I was deprived of anything. About the time I started school, Mom was hired as the postmaster for the tiny post office in Avalon and was able to obtain a loan to buy the house that was my home until I left for college and then married.

About that loan, I'll share a short bit of information to remind my readers of how far women have come in the last 70 years. These days, if you have a job, a decent credit history, and a bit of collateral, it isn't too difficult to get a housing loan. But at the time I was born women were not, as a rule, a common factor in the work force. As a result of their role as temporary replacements for servicemen in factories and other jobs during WWII this was beginning to change.

But my mother had no credit history, no collateral, and in spite of having the postmaster position, was not able to obtain a house loan from any of the financial institutions in nearby Chillicothe. She came home in tears one day, bitter over the unfairness of the discrimination simply because she was not a man. It was only after her brother agreed to co–sign that she was able to get the loan.

Thereafter, she applied for and obtained credit cards for Sears, Roebuck and Company and Montgomery Ward mail order companies. That's how she did most of our shopping for clothes, appliances, and Christmas presents as long as she lived. When I was a senior in high school she was adamant that I go to the local J.C. Penney store and apply for a credit card so I could start building a credit history. And following her frugal example, I was careful not to spend beyond my ability to repay and have always avoided credit charges by paying off the balance each month. Thanks, Mom!

So that was one of the first of my life lessons that have helped me over the years. Another valuable life lesson that came out of my early life was the fact that life is not a guaranteed or permanent condition. But more on that later.

What is the Meaning of Life?

Human ego is all encompassing. It's mostly about us, now. Likely not one in a thousand people would ever admit to considering their life as the ephemeral thing it is against the backdrop of evolutionary history. It's hard enough to appreciate the cycles of human social, cultural, economic and technological development, let alone admit that our existence is just a drop in the bucket of all that has gone before or is yet to come. Or not come, as the case may be, in the event that some fool decides to "drop the big one," in which additional case this writing is moot. But I digress…. With hopefulness that we may indeed be around for a few generations. I thought I might share some ruminations that keep kicking around in my brain about my own progress along the road of life. Considering how the years have flown, it feels now like that road has been a trip at turnpike speed, but it didn't feel like that when it started. As a kid it seemed like all those things I looked forward to—Christmas, birthdays, summer vacations—would never come. Not only did time creep, but the future was a big white impenetrable cloud of nowhere, a big "Who knows?"

Only in these last few years has it become apparent that, indeed, I am not going to live forever. Do I feel stupid, or what? And now when I feel I'm running out of time I begin to appreciate and to think more about the past., and not just my past. I started digging into my ancestry, then I began to do more reading about history in general. Eventually I found myself back where I started—thinking about life.

I have finally come to the personally opinionated conclusion that there is no "meaning of life." But in the larger sense, my belief is that life just *is*. As that famous quotation goes, "Out of all the gin joints in all the towns in all the world...", I might paraphrase it to say that out of all the planets in all the galaxies in all the universe, how is it that this tiny planet happened to give rise to this thing we call life? That is possibly what makes us keep trying to give life meaning, trying to understand.

LIFE'S A CRAZY QUILT

Who and what are we?
Clipped from the patchwork of time,
One square of all the blanket weave makes sense.
The rest is patternless.

Seeking to define, analyze, model,
We lose our life's design,
thinking to weave our own.
Only one form shows through.

The shape our life assumes
depends not on our own precepts
but on the niche we fill for others, and
on how we fit the finished work.

Death

Ah, what a morbid topic! Or is it? One usually thinks of morbidity as death, but actually, when I looked up the definition of morbid, the first definition given was "akin to, related to, or characteristic of disease." So I suppose the second definition would be more appropriate—"abnormally susceptible to or characterized by gloomy or unwholesome feelings." So maybe I don't want to use the term morbidity after all, because I don't now and have never felt that way about death.

As a biologist and life–long naturalist, I always thought of death as a natural outcome, because as the saying goes, "None of us are getting out of here alive," in spite of wishful thinking on the part of humankind since the dawn of intelligent thought. We refuse to face the indignity that the world can and will get along without us. Ha!

So instead of considering death itself, perhaps it would be more appropriate to think about the human reaction to death. It is also obvious that one's reaction would be to the death of others, and not our own, since when you're dead, well….

Enough philosophy. On to the more personal stuff. And if you are not into morbidity, you might just want to skip the rest of this writing.

My Experience with Death

Open caskets were and still are a common part of funerals, and as a kid I saw a lot of dead people. This was before the inclusion of seat belts in vehicles, and rural roads, both paved and unpaved, were dangerous at high speed, narrow with lots of curves. Boys being boys, once they got a car there was only one way to drive—go like the devil! There was also a lot of drinking, so needless to say there were a lot of folks who didn't make it home.

Besides dead people, rural kids were and still are exposed to at lot of other dead critters. I saw lots of pets get run over, chickens beheaded by sundry means, birds met their end by ubiquitous B–B guns, etcetera, etcetera. But again, when you're young it just doesn't hit home. We observed, were sad, but death was an accepted fact and the example we had from adults was that you grieved and then you got on with things. At that time, my parents and grandparents generation had experienced a lot of death.

I first experienced death through the grief of my mother, who lost her father from heart disease, her husband by lung cancer, and brother–in–law, Dad's brother, within a single year. I was only three years old when my father passed, so I have little memory of him, and I have only a vague memory of my grandfather Van in a large wicker wheelchair.

Uncle Lester I remember for more personal reasons. He was afflicted with a condition called Buerger disease, not much encountered these days. This morbidity results in the loss of circulation to the extremities, leading, for him, to amputation of hands and lower legs as the disease progressed. He lived with Dad's sister Opal and her husband. To get around the house he used a kitchen chair with caster wheels fitted to the bottom, which he managed pretty well as he propelled himself along walls and through doors. He had clothespins taped to the stubs of his arms that enabled him to use utensils at the table, and even use a screwdriver and other tools to disassemble and repair the industrial sewing machine in his bedroom. The reason his memory is so clear to me is because he used to take me on rides through the house sitting on the rungs of the chair bottom. I was so charmed.

As a consequence of being a change–of–life child, many of the people in my mother's life were older, and were contemporaries of her mother. In our rural community everyone pretty much knew everyone else, and when deaths occurred quite a few neighbors were present. Funerals were pretty frequent, given the population of older folks and the questionable health of many who lived through some rough years. I saw plenty of open–casket funerals, so I was accustomed to the idea of death, to the tears and grief of mourners.

Death as Entertainment

During the course of my life, I have always been a member of some sort of club—and I use the term loosely—that definition being "a group identified by some common characteristic." The first was our local 4–H club, the Avalon Busy Bees! The second was the Columbia Record Club, which I joined in high school and kept up into college as long as I could afford it on a student budget. I had a somewhat eclectic taste in music and still have some great vinyl from those years.

But my most enduring clubs through the years have been book clubs, as in "buy books." I read and have always read so much and so fast that I never had the patience to sit down with a group of people and actually discuss or dissect what I read, because by the time everyone else was through with a book, I was a dozen or so past it and it was old stuff.

I progressed from one interest to another over the years, from horses and mystery, through sci–fi and mystery, into westerns and mystery, and espionage and mystery, archaeology, war, historic fiction and detective mystery, and most recently a genre referred to as cozy mysteries—cute bakery/book club/ knitting–quilting–antique and art store who–done–its. And mysteries usually include one or more deaths.

Well, I occasionally sneak in some actual history, science and nature, and sort of educational stuff but, as you can probably guess, I'm not much into books on self–help, politics, romance, or (with rare exceptions), biographies.

Well, that was certainly a digression! What I wanted to talk about was the books I discovered along the way about the subject of death. History documents the morbid (there it is again!) interest by the public in circumstances causing, surrounding, or personifying death. Stephen King refers to it as the "let's stop and look at the accident" syndrome. In spite of the gruesome, horrific, bloody facts, the public in general likes to be shocked.

One book that stands out in my mind was entitled The Wisconsin Death Trip. It is a collection of essays and photographs documenting a century or more of public fascination with the weird and macabre. For instance, when outlaws were shot and killed, their corpses were publicly displayed in coffins, blood and all. Death photos of infants abound; there are even one or two in my family albums. Many photos of lynchings and public hangings show a crowd of people standing around gaping or picnicking nearby. Talk about morbid!

These days, with improvements in health and public safety, the causes and nature of deaths have changed. Worldwide, deaths due to war, disease, and starvation are still common and extensive, mainly in third–world countries. By contrast, in the United States the most prevalent causes of death by far are those associated with chronic health problems, which are in turn due to of unhealthy diets, obesity, and increased longevity. Multiple forms of cancer, heart and circulatory disease, diabetes, for example, have always been with us, but as life expectancy increases there is more time for these organic diseases to develop. And in spite of the advances in preventing and treating infectious disease, it seems that we have simply traded the older germs for some newer ones.

And sadly, deaths by gun violence are increasingly common, and fewer people these days seem to be intrigued or titillated by these, other than the news media which still manage to make a lot of money and prolong our distress with their coverage. Maybe we are finally getting over our morbid fascination with death and will replace it with a more respectful, gentler response. And no doubt we will always wonder what comes after.

When I Die

I don't obsess on my own death, but I have been giving some thought as to the disposition of my remains. I haven't yet really come to any definite conclusion. There are really not a whole lot of options, given that someone else is going to have to see that it gets done.

They don't like dead bodies on scaffolds these days, although it does have some appeal. It's pretty easy, also inexpensive. Plus it gives loved ones time to get used to the fact of your demise. However, I think it is probably illegal, plus, given the difficulty of finding a suitable location away from public sight and, you know, some people would be grossed out. As if I would care.

In some countries they throw you (oops, lay you) on a big fire and your ashes fly off into the air, and the minerals—what DO they do with the minerals? But that contributes to global warming, plus that is also not a local option.

One of the most common options is burial. And if you are going to be buried, you have to be embalmed. Nasty stuff, so you don't rot and pollute the groundwater. I mean, who are they preserving the remains for? Nobody wants to keep them at home.

Also, people rarely get dug up again, and think of all the good nutrients in a body that are locked away and do nobody any good! Really! I mean dead animals get made into fertilizer and leather and other useful products. In my humble and probably irreverent opinion, humans are probably the most useless and detrimental life form on earth. We need to get over ourselves!

Sorry. I sometimes get carried away. Where was I...?

I really always did want to be buried unpreserved in a wooden box under a big tree, where the roots could use me for food and I would become wood, or leaves, or nuts. But forget that. I also thought about donating my body to science, but then there's that nasty embalming again.

I have just about settled on cremation. I talked it over with my family, and they are pretty much okay with whatever I decide. Most of my family are buried in the cemetery near my hometown of Avalon, Missouri, and there's room there in their plot if I want it. I told both my girls to just spread my dust over the ground there. Their only comment was, "Can we keep some of the ashes?" I'm curious as to what they plan to do with them.

I'm also curious as to where I would want my spirit to go if it's going to hang around for a good long while. Given what my life has been, I don't feel called to any other plane of existence. I don't think I've been bad enough for the hot place, and how can heaven be any better than Mother Earth?

Finally, although I'm somewhat dubious but also intrigued by the concept of reincarnation, that might be an interesting experience. Maybe I'll do that.

WAKE ME WHEN I DIE

What has death to do with me?
I walk in sunshine, moonlight, starbright.
Even in the depths of earth or black of darkest night,
Life is what I breathe, not death.

The pulse of time beats in my mind
And drives the thoughts that give me breath.
It's fear of nothingness that makes us blind,
That lays a darkness on the soul.

So many die in life,
Giving up the freedom of their thoughts,
Victim of the social reform knife
That castrates intellect and renders action impotent.
The questioner, the young and virile searcher after truth,
Labeled by authority as radical and malcontent.
We bleed our greatest asset in its youth.

Not I to spend my life in prostrate adoration
To the gods of duty, nor in solemn piety,
Nor offer up as sacrifice my soul
In abstinence, nor practicing sobriety.

I intend to live life to its limits,
Taste the cups that pass my way,
Extend my heart to all who need,
Not waste a single minute of a single day.

And if I lose the physical integrity
Of my independent and irreverent self
And have the great audacity to die,
Don't put my memory on a shelf.

Wake me where I lie upon or in the ground,
With wild and raucous laughter, love, and song.
Drink strong spirits from the bottle and the earth and sky
And talk about me. I won't be gone long.

A MODEL FOR MY TOMBSTONE

Carved in stone, the hawk perches
Atop a granite tree,
Tearing apart a graven mouse,
Its wings half spread for balance,
Cruel and beautiful,
            an epitaph to life.

Each creature lives
By an ordered pattern,
And each in its turn dies,
Its substance given up
            to other creature processes.

Place this stone above my resting place,
So that in death
My reverence for the natural order
Is expressed,
Just as my verse had held
            the essence of my living.

D Canote

WHEN I DIE—SOME SCENARIOS

Number One:

In case the subject arises,
If you bury me I want
A plain ash box, sanded but no varnish.
Tung oil finish would be nice.

Planted like a seed
Beneath a big noisy tree (not pine),
I'd like to hear the leaves in summer,
The wind through empty limbs in winter,

And friends to meet above my grave.
Thanatopsis – I think I'd hear that
From beyond the boundary.
Songs of fellowship and life.

Speak of anything you want, I've heard it all,
It won't make any difference to me.
Only you who remain behind
Will have to suffer now.

Number Two:

Having some second thoughts about the disposal of my remains. They won't
let a body rot just anywhere, groundwater and all that.
So natural burial doesn't appear to be an option,
In spite of all the 'dead' germs we probably drank as kids from our town cisterns.
And they won't let you rot above ground, because that would highly offend a
lot of noses, indigenous people be damned.
So maybe I'll let them burn me up. It was good enough for the Vikings and the
people of India, but wait....
Does that constitute air pollution? Contribute to global climate change?
So OK, maybe I'll go with cremation, the least offensive and the cheapest.
Just see that at least some of my ashes are spread across the graves of my
family in my old home town.
And let my kids keep the rest. But I still hope there'll be a party, and fair warning...
I plan to attend.

73

Passages and Transitions

Some of my most profound thinking is on road trips. Maybe profound isn't the right word. Insightful? Okay, let me start over. I do a lot of thinking on road trips. Especially when I'm traveling alone. When I'm around other people there always seems to be a lot of talking going on. Not that conversation is bad, at least when it is thoughtful, stimulating, entertaining, yada, yada. And being retired I have a lot of quiet time at home to think, reminisce, all that. But there is something about driving along, watching the passing scenery, seeing something new, that kicks my mind into the vaults of my past and triggers connections, insights, and introspection.

Life's a Journey?

I wonder, are other people's lives like mine? I asked myself the other day, "What kind of changes have I been through since my life began all those years ago in Chicago?" I once heard a description of a person's existence as a cylindrical object like a roll of salami, with a slice through the roll seen as a moment in time, each slice an hour, minute, or day in the life. We're born at one end of the roll and cease to live at the other end.

I really like that explanation, and I can visualize my life as a road trip, the slices all the events of the trip, all the rest stops and the experiences and people I have met along the way. I can even imagine the road with occasional tunnels, passageways between one stage and the next, sort of like Alice down the rabbit hole. Wow! I never knew when I started in one end of a tunnel where I would come out.

Stages

I loved school. The smell of old wood floors, chalk dust, the taste of paste, reading books, what's not to love? With three grades in one room, one teacher, we naturally got tracked by ability. Three of us—Ross, Leon, and I—always finished our assignments first and got the privilege of the chalkboard. Located along one long wall of the room and at a height suitable for short legs, it was perfect for drawing scenarios that would have made great comic books. I drew mostly trees and flowers, snakes, bugs, and spiders, while Ross and Leon created battles between cowboys and indians or soldiers, tanks, and explosions. I so wish someone had taken photos.

Up until junior high we got lots of recess time to blow off steam. I don't remember much about elementary school, other than occasional chain reaction vomiting episodes. Usually not me, because I never ate enough to be sick. And junior high was pretty forgettable too. Probably full of the usual mindless social adjustments and indoctrination from teachers trying to mold young minds into responsible adults. Ha!

High school was a different matter. I won't elaborate on the trials and tribulations of a young girl going through puberty, because if you're female, you know what I'm talking about, and if you're male you had your own problems. But the memorable part was that school went from being a formulaic process of rote learning and indoctrination to having one's mind stretched by more interesting stuff.

For me, the challenge of math beyond arithmetic and the science behind mechanics and within cells was a revelation. I was like a kid in a candy store—where to look first! Even the mechanics of writing—sentence structure, reading and writing poetry, and introduction to world literature—was lovely and appealed to my innate desire for order and structure. Through those four years I was fortunate to have a suite of very stimulating, competent and charismatic teachers. In a small school with a typical class size of twenty to thirty students, teachers had plenty of time for individual instruction and most had a genuine liking for kids.

Finally, I have to say that socially, the kind of cliques and peer pressure so common in that age group was virtually nonexistent for us. We occasionally switched best friends, both male and female, rarely had harsh words or arguments, and stood up for each other when things were rough. That may have been because of the years of familiarity as we passed through the grade levels together, or simply the result of the closeness and acceptance of a rural community. Whatever it was, it gave me the confidence and character that enabled me to leave my small part of the world and step eagerly, if somewhat tentatively, into my future.

Transitions

It is probably a truism and inevitable that we change over the years as a result of new experiences, life lessons, and the challenges of making our way in the world. I suppose there are some who go through life without moving into the world, without learning much more about themselves or their context in the scheme of things. I believe that without significant challenges we can never experience any significant transitions and growth. But I doubt there are many who can say that they are unchanged throughout their lives.

My first major transition was pretty common, similar to many of my generation. Off to college I went to earn a diploma and become a teacher. Along the way I was somewhat sidetracked by a marriage proposal, which I accepted, but which did not interfere with the diploma getting. My husband was also a teacher, was in fact my senior high school chemistry teacher. (And no, we did not date before I graduated; in fact there were several 'significant others' before him.) I do recall with amusement that the wags about town followed with interest the amount of time before our first daughter was born—four years, the longest pregnancy on record!

We taught, farmed, and reared two daughters from our home near Marshall, Missouri up until the point when I went back to school to earn a graduate degree. At that time I had reached the top of my salary schedule and, realizing that I could not advance beyond that step without additional education, I enrolled at the University of Missouri – Columbia.. Eventually the 60–mile commute and personal factors within our marriage led to a divorce, and I moved to Columbia to finish my degree.

A Hiatus and New Horizons

Throughout the course of my teaching career I taught Biology, Chemistry, Physics, Anatomy and Physiology, and Environment Science, so by the time I was ready for grad school, I was well prepared for my GREs and interested in new fields of study. At that time my husband and I were farming, so rather than continue in the direction of Education, I pursued and earned a Masters in Agronomy. Research in agro–chemicals diverted my attention to additional studies in Fisheries and Wildlife. I didn't return immediately to teaching but worked for ten years doing research in environmental chemistry and was finally employed doing corporate aquatic toxicity testing in support of industrial product registration.

Those years which I call my "middle years" are chronicled, in part, in my previous books. I will just say briefly that these were years of personal growth and discovery, a period during which my circle of friends and colleagues expanded hugely, and

I was introduced to so many new experiences and vistas that I couldn't help but be changed in ways I never imagined.

Graduate school was followed by a return to the work force. After several years in the fields of cancer research and toxicology, I returned to teaching. It turns out I have a bit more to say about that.

What it Means to be a Teacher

Of all the passages I traversed throughout my life, the most important to me, and the one that most fulfilled me was the period of years during which I was a teacher. In a moment of enlightenment, I realized that being a teacher was the essence of who I had become. Like a singer bursting into song, or a dancer moving into action when music is heard, given the proper question I find myself back in teacher mode, spewing forth a gusher of facts and explanations.

Why Teaching?

When my mother announced that I *would* go to college and earn a teaching certificate "...because they will always need teachers!" I started as an English major, since that was where I made my best grades. After a semester of diagramming sentences and critiquing Madam Bovary, I was bored out of my skull and looked around,

so to speak, for a new direction. What classes did I *really* enjoy in school? What would challenge my interest and aptitudes? Aha! Science! When I came home and told my mom I was changing my major/minor to Biology and Chemistry, she looked at me in astonishment and asked, "Can you do that?"—meaning did I think I was capable of those disciplines? Somewhat surprised, I answered yes, I thought so. That launched my career as a scientist.

When I began my teaching career in 1968, Missouri's educational system had not yet been placed under the political scrutiny that it endures today. The previous year's movies included what I considered both an inspiration and a warning for my chosen profession. The movie, *Up the Down Staircase*, starred a young Sandy Dennis as a beginning English teacher in an overcrowded New York public high school. It was thoroughly satisfying as an inspirational and entertaining film, and little did I guess that much of the facts and portrayals would become familiar to me in my own career.

Preparing to begin my teaching career was in a way like preparing to become a first-time parent. I knew in an abstract way what to expect, but nothing can prepare you for the reality. Working with the adolescent personality was another form of an education. As for academic preparation, a science teacher in small-town schools was expected to teach all the science classes, including physics. "Physics?" I responded in horror to my principal when he so informed me. "I've only had one five-hour class in college physics!" He said, "Well, that's all you need." That began my evolution as a self–taught instructor of subjects for which I had little training.

My first teaching job was in a small town with Kindergarten through twelfth grade. Science and Math classrooms were located in the basement next to the boiler room. Anything that blew up would have taken out the entire high school population. On my very first day of teaching, I was prepared with lesson plans, textbooks, class rolls, and a brand new schoolteacher dress. The classroom had a fresh coat of paint on the concrete floor, ground floor windows with no shades, an old oak office desk and antique office chair on casters, one of which was loose.

As the first–hour bell rang, my students filed in quietly and filled their seats, watching expectantly as I remained seated at my desk, leaning forward and smiling in welcome. The tardy bell rang and I leaned back, preparing to rise and take roll. As I did so, I had forgotten about the loose caster, which fell off as I was leaning forward. The chair promptly fell sideways, dumping me out onto the floor. I slowly picked myself up, brushing off and straightening my clothing. I looked down at the chair, then up at my class, asking, "Now, which one of you took the roller off my chair?"

The students, a class of ninth graders, looked at me in stupefaction for a few seconds. Then as I started laughing they also started giggling. I thought to myself, "What a way to start a career!"

Nothing scared me about teaching until many years later. However, I began eventually to feel stagnated and in need of some new inspiration. After twelve years, having reached the top of the salary schedule, I was ineligible for further salary increases without an advanced degree, so I left teaching to work on my Masters at the University of Missouri–Columbia.

Finally, after seventeen years away from teaching, I found myself yearning again for the classroom. Near the end of the summer of 1997 I learned of an opening in Science at a local high school. There had been a few applicants throughout the summer but evidently none met the approval of the administration. Although I had some reservations, I decided to apply.

It was August, one week before classes were scheduled to commence, and I received a call from the Science Department Chairman ask me to come by for an interview. When I showed up, we did some informal chatting, took a tour of the building and science classrooms, and I followed along with an odd tingling numbness in my extremities, and a sense of disorientation, wondering, "What in the world am I doing?" I was experiencing the first panic attack of my life.

On Friday, I was hired. I had no idea how to navigate the hallways, knew none of the staff or faculty, and had no lesson plans when I showed up on Monday. Two days of orientation and I was once again a teacher. Nearly every morning for the next month, as I drove to school I had more panic attacks, but they finally disappeared, and I was back in the groove.

David H. Hickman High School was at that time one of Columbia's three city high schools, housing nearly 2000 students in tenth through twelfth grades. It wasn't New York City, but in all respects was a great deal bigger that the small rural schools of my earlier years. The student body was likewise a much different animal (if you will forgive the phrase) than I was used to. The cross section of the student body represented a wide spectrum of cultural, socioeconomic, and educational backgrounds. Inner city students, foreign students, children of doctors, lawyers, university professors, farmers, factory and office workers, as well as the homeless, unemployed, and incarcerated—all traveled the same halls and occupied the same classrooms.

In spite of my initial uncertainties, the ten years I spent teaching Biology, Chemistry, and Environmental Science at

Hickman were my most memorable as a teacher. Through interactions with my fellow teachers and classes, I unexpectedly learned some things about myself I didn't know. I learned to take each day as a challenge and an adventure (some were, of course, a much greater challenge than others), and to make no assumptions about the individuals who walked into my classroom. They were blank slates that I had the privilege to write on, works of art that I could help discover; and my greatest hopes were that they would take away with them something interesting, inspiring, or useful.

A Career Like No Other

Describing what it means to be a teacher is like trying to describe a rummage sale. Or as Forest Gump's mom would say, "...like a box of chocolates. You never know what you're going to get." That goes for pretty much everything associated with teaching, from the support you get from your administrators, to the working relationships with fellow teachers, to the physical infrastructure of the school and your classroom, to the variety in the makeup of your classes. Sure, I know people could say, "Yes, but that's true of all jobs," but what is so amazingly unique, and not like any other workplace, is the character of children and adolescents.

Parents of multiple children can appreciate that not only are no two siblings are alike, but some are so different as to cause observers, or even the parents, to question their origin. Expand that thought to the student population of a school and even a single classroom. Even in small rural schools there is a wide diversity with respect to ethnic and socioeconomic factors.

From the day a child walks into their first classroom, their whole life is altered. For a period of each day the teacher is called upon to act in place of the parent in nurturing, disciplining, and inspiring students while filling their brains with facts—building reading, language, and math skills that will form the basis for success when they are adults. A teacher is also expected to turn out individuals who are good, well–rounded citizens, respectful of others, able to cope with challenges and, now more importantly (to the Department of Elementary and Secondary Education), to successfully pass state–mandated standardized tests.

Consider further the young person who walks into the classroom each day. And believe me when I say that for a teacher the term "my classroom" is a very territorial concept. For the elementary teacher, the child is pretty much a blank slate, a piece of clay, with a mind mostly void of preconceptions, who is more or less pliable and receptive to new experiences. Those children are our children for that period of their day and week they are under our supervision. We care deeply about their well–being and our greatest desire is for them to achieve their greatest potential under our care and tutelage. But they are not all equally capable in terms of innate intelligence or preparation for the classroom.

Early childhood education is one of the most significant areas of curriculum improvement in recent years. Early access to books, being read to, and introduced at an early age to numbers and problem solving goes a long way toward ensuring success in the classroom. It is not in the cards that all children will be equally nurtured at home, or that they will all have positive attitudes toward education.

As a high school teacher, I have always had great respect for elementary teachers who are required and mostly able to deal with occasional grubby, unwashed bodies, snotty noses, occasional or frequent up–chucks, and toilet accidents. Generally when kids get to adolescence they are past the worst of those and what I dealt with was a different suite of issues—snotty attitudes, potty mouths, and a wide range of inappropriate sartorial choices that sometimes require interventions. Those, of course, are the negative issues and, for me at least, there were plenty of positive rewards in teaching that far outweighed the negatives.

When I finally retired from teaching, there was a period of withdrawal and, not to say guilt, exactly; but for some time I experienced days when I was uncomfortable, feeling that there was somewhere I should be, something I should be doing. I would still find myself waking in the middle of the night having profound insights into exactly how I should introduce a new lesson, what hands–on experiment I could add to suck my students into a science concept.

These days that guilt has dissipated and I certainly don't miss getting up before the sun to get to the classroom, or the hours of grading, or the demands of seemingly purposeless administrative hoops. But I still occasionally have those nighttime brainstorms, along with periodic dreams of the classroom. I was having lunch recently with a group of retired Hickman teachers, when the subject of school dreams came up. It seems we all had, and still have, the same ones in common. "School has started and I can't find my classroom." "I walk into the classroom and have no textbooks or lesson plans." "I don't have a class schedule and don't know what I'm teaching." "My class is out of control and won't listen to me." And the most common, "I'm at school / in the hall / in my classroom with no clothes on!"

But I do still miss the teaching, the interactions with those young minds (the ones that were awake at least), the satisfaction, as my brother Jerry, also a schoolteacher, would say, of fighting the good fight, and of watching the lights at the end of the tunnel come on.

Back to the Garden

After a final interesting and rewarding ten years of teaching, I was ready for a new adventure. That was when I transitioned into a market gardener. For those of you who garden, you know the joy of planting, harvesting, and eating from your garden. We love the smell of the soil, the beauty of watching things grow, flower, and fruit, and even the blisters and aching muscles at the end of a day provide some satisfaction and evidence of accomplishment.

But market gardening is a business and does not allow the luxury of taking a day off when there are gardens to tend, weeds to conquer, and produce to be picked. Timing the picking for optimum quality, as well as getting the crops to market without loss is tricky. And that doesn't include the loading and getting up before the hairy crack of dawn to get to market and set up. I'll just end by saying that, in keeping with what I told my husband, James when I started, I did it as long as is was fun and worth the effort, and when it stopped being fun, I quit.

Basil

Ocimum
basilieum

D. Canote

Since then I have what I hope is my last transition. I went back to some of the activities I enjoyed in the years before I became so occupied with making a living. Several years ago I took up the hobby of watercolor painting, the product of which now accompanies my writing. And I took up writing, the result of which is this and my previous two books of essays. And last but not least, I returned to the sewing skills that I learned as a girl in 4–H and high school Home Economics. At my request, my friend Edie taught me how to hand–piece and quilt, a skill my mother and grandmother also practiced, and which reconnects me to their lives.

Aging

I was sitting in the kitchen this morning, reading one in a long sequence of the murder mysteries that keep me occupied these days. Like most fiction stories I read, this one had the requisite love scene and, as I read, I was distracted by thoughts of love stories of my earlier life.

In the face of the realities of aging daily thrust upon me I know those experiences are now only memories. There is some relief in the fact that as I grow older, the angst of romantic relationships is left behind and I am able to think rationally about the feelings that once drove me to distraction. And yet, the best of those feelings and thoughts still linger in body memory. Like an unexpected scent, I am suddenly catapulted into a moment in time when the feel of skin on skin, the warmth of a lover's breath and arms are everything, and the yearning to relive those moments is almost unbearable.

The only transition I'm having these days is from an active to a sedentary life, thanks to certain limitations of age. My biggest challenge is trying to grow old gracefully.

How is it possible that I have gotten so old! "Oh well," someone says, "people are living longer now and you still have lots of good years left." And I just want to smack them up side the head and say, like my Aunt Pauline once told me "You just wait!"

INTEGRATION, EMPATHY AND TRANSPOSITION

Consummated, summated,
Life from birth to death
Is more than the sum of the parts,
And you and I,
Body mind and soul together,
Must decide where integration starts.

If we cannot perceive
The workings of the world
With conscious logic in our brain,
We can still feel
The force that rises, falls, and flows,
And live a portion of each other's joy and pain.

And in the process,
Putting life together,
Seeing through a different pair of eyes,
We will become
A bird of different feather
And like the phoenix, from the ashes rise.

Chapter Six
Poems

The Sportsman

How wondrous is his great pursuit
With dog and gun, or rod and lure,
Ignores discomforts for his cause,
Heat, wet, and cold he will endure.

The cunning bird and wily fish
Cannot elude his frying pan.
He seeks what runs, or flies, or swims.
He will outwit them if he can.

How great the hunt! How strong the call
That draws him from his daily tasks.
To go alone into the wild
And stalk his food is all he asks.

For what he seeks, the meat he takes,
Is not alone his final goal.
He takes communion with himself
And feeds his universal soul.

Solitary

Some days I sit
Muffled in an insulating void
While all around me
People speak and move
And never notice
I'm not there

It's like being indoors
On a rainy day
Miserable with a cold
While others splash around outside
Laughing, singing
Getting wet and having fun

The Hunt

I rose up from my bed before the dawn
And went to wait to kill a deer.
Through frosted grass and crystal air,
Among deluded trees and down the hill
I stumbled through my sleep.

I waited for the sun and watched the light
As morning grew around me, and
I thought about the thing I came to do,
While jays sat up above and disapproved
Each time I rearranged my frozen feet.

Booming echoes sounded through the valley
As the light increased, and still
I sat and waited on the rock
Until the rumbling of my stomach
Rivaled noises from the hunters' guns.

I left and ate and later
Came again back to my rock.
As afternoon passed on I watched until at last
The passage of sun behind the hill
Left hard cold edges on the air,

And no deer came that day to die.

Rio Sabrinas

Speak to me.
Speak to me
Of quiet places where the heart can go
To lay the sorrow of its living down,
Where silent pools absorb the thought
And give back no reflection of the mind,
Where morning scintillates with songs
Of other lives.

Speak to me.
Speak to me
Of golden days with no demands
And nights of solitary sleep,
Of mornings new and evenings cool,
And nothing to confuse the truths
That nature speaks so freely
To the heart that listens.

Speak to me.
Speak to me.
I wish to hear your thoughts
And know the secret yearnings of your life.
Allow me entrance to your mind,
The evenings and the mornings of your soul,
That I can live another life
In quiet places.

Experiment

He didn't like me from the start,
The scruffy little ball of fur,
But pity nibbled at my heart
And found a weak spot, as it were,
    And so, more fool, I took him in.

Sentimental do–gooder that I was,
I didn't have the sense to see
That this black, mangy pile of fuzz
Was going to be the ruin of me.
    I thought, "At last I have a roommate!"

Within a week he'd named himself.
After running into doors
And knocking dishes off the shelf
And leaving presents on the floor,
    I'd hear myself, "Hey, shit–for–brains…!"

My three–pound oscar disappeared
Out of his tank, I searched the floor
And found a clean–picked pile of bones
In a neat bunch behind the door.
    I thought, "This isn't turning out so good."

He'd lie in wait, docile and sweet,
Until he knew my toes were bare,
Then jump out and attack my feet,
A pounce–and–bite–and–run affair.
    I got so I slept in my shoes.

He'd get me in a purple funk.
I'd throw him out, he'd come back in.
One night I thought, "I'll get him drunk."
I dumped his water, put in gin.
    He paid me back by giving back his dinner on my bed.

My sleep was wrecked. I'd hear a scream
And wake up with two wild red eyes
Glaring like a nightmare dream.
By now I wasn't too surprised
    At anything the damn fool pervert cat would do.

He ran out in the street one day,
A big fast semi smashed him flat.
I left him there 'til he was dry.
My brother calls him "sail cat."
    He makes a better frisbee than he did a roommate.

Another Wall

There are a cohort of us
Who didn't go to war.
I'm not talking about
The ones who were too old
Or too young or ill,
Or crippled or insane,
Or that unclassified bunch
That simple avoided it
One way or another.
My group was caught
In the multi–jawed vise
Of Victorian strength and morals
And the free–thinking 60s,
Between the ERA and the awareness
Of a liberated middle age,
And I tell you,
We know the wall within.

We felt the injustice
That men should have to go
To fight and kill and die
(For something that might
Or might not be worth it),
While we went safely on with life,
Learning, working, growing,
Playing and loving,

Risking neither our lives
Nor our souls.
And when we began to hear
And see on TV and in the movies
And in books, the stories
Of what happened to
Our brothers and husbands,
Friends and lovers,
We questioned how significant
Were our lives and
What moral strength we gained
By staying home.
And something made us want
To reach out further in the wold
And give something back to it.

But when we reach
We find our own wall,
A barrier we cannot look behind,
Built of a hundred different bricks.
Never pick up a hitchhiker
Or interfere with someone beating their dog.
Status bricks, like
How many asses you had to kiss
To get your own house,
And by God you'd better not
Put a door ding in my new Volvo

Or shortcut across my lawn.
Some are bricks of sheer ignorance,
Others a lack of the courage of conviction, or
Of any conviction at all.
Blind–eyed bricks that
Never see the world,
Or smell the wet earth in spring,
Or sunshine on their own skin.
And then there is the cement
Of our own fear of failure
That fills in the seams
And makes it so hard to tear down.

Well, brothers,
I'll say this to you,
Who went and fought
And wounded or lost your souls.
There are some of us
Who didn't go, but share
The darkness of your nights,
Your horror and hatred
Of the futility and waste of war
And would speak, if we knew how,
The words to heal your wounds
And touch you with our love,
And share the common hope we hold,
The garden behind the wall.

www.ingramcontent.com/pod-product-compliance
Lightning Source LLC
Chambersburg PA
CBHW041528150426

42812CB00059BA/2665